The Fifty-first in France

THE GILDED STATUE OF THE CAMPANILE OF THE ÉGLISE NOTRE DAME DE BREBIERES, ALBERT

Frontispiece.

THE FIFTY-FIRST IN FRANCE

BY
CAPTAIN ROBERT B. ROSS
GORDON HIGHLANDERS

ILLUSTRATED BY JESSIE K. ROSS

DEDICATION

TO THE MEMORY

OF

MY FALLEN COMRADES

PREFACE

I DESIRE to thank the many friends who by kind words of counsel and encouragement have helped me to write this book of reminiscences. In particular my thanks are due to Mr. D. M. Watt, of the *Ross-shire Journal*, for his permission to incorporate a few articles from my pen which appeared in that paper under the title of " A Ross-shire Gordon Highlander's Diary of the War."

R. B. R.

ALNESS,
1918.

CONTENTS

PART I
FROM MAY TO DECEMBER 1915

CHAPTER I
	PAGE
FAIR STOOD THE WIND FOR FRANCE . .	19

CHAPTER II
TOMMY AND HIS TRENCH 46

CHAPTER III
THE FIRST SHOT 66

CHAPTER IV
THE SILENT GUNS 84

CHAPTER V
EXTENDING THE LINE 106

CHAPTER VI
PILGRIMS IN PICARDY 128

CONTENTS

PART II
MAY TO NOVEMBER 1916

CHAPTER VII
MINES AND MISERIES	PAGE 173

CHAPTER VIII
IN THE WAKE OF THE PUSH . . . 198

CHAPTER IX
HIGH WOOD 215

CHAPTER X
A CITY IN CELLARS 239

CHAPTER XI
THE GENERATION OF CAIN . . . 260

CHAPTER XII
AN ARMY ON LEASH 288

CHAPTER XIII
BEAUMONT-HAMEL 303

ILLUSTRATIONS

The Gilded Statue of the Campanile of the Église Notre Dame de Brebieres, Albert	*Frontispiece*
	PAGE
Disembarkation	20
A Ruined Farmhouse near Richebourg	76
Arras	88
The Church of Estaires and the River Lys	104
The Smoke of Battle	116
Thiepval Château before the War	152
La Boisselle	168
Mont St. Eloi	184
The Spectral Skeleton of Fricourt Château, now a Heap of Powdered Bricks	224
St. Omer	240
The Somme at Abbeville	264
Hébuterne	280
Near Mailly-Maillet	288

"Hence the Faith and Fire within us,
    Men who march away
    Ere the barn-cocks say
    Night is growing grey,
To hazards whence no tears can win us;
Hence the Faith and Fire within us,
    Men who march away."
THOMAS HARDY.

Part I—From May to December 1915

I   FAIR STOOD THE WIND FOR FRANCE

ON the third day of May in the year of our Lord nineteen hundred and fifteen, the seventh battalion of the Gordon Highlanders paraded for the last time on English soil. The companies marched to their appointed stations, every breast aching with pride and hopes realised at last. All the windows were lined with spectators, and not a few women were in tears. While the men were being marshalled and dressed, and until the rifles had come clattering down to the order, there was a sympathetic silence among the populace. At 6.30 Colonel Bower rode up. The adjutant saluted with that peculiar salute of his which could not have been expressly called half-casual, but which had such individuality that it could never have been associated with any other officer. The battalion came to attention. The final commands were rapped out. Three drum-beats, and the pipes blew with a fiercer assurance than ever. Our good-byes were parched upon our lips, for Bedford had mothered us and we had grown up as her own children.

At Ampthill military siding a dense crowd had assembled to witness the departure of the troops. The men sang and whistled with fervour. Their enthusiasm was so contagious that cheeks yet glistening with tears were now wrinkled with smiles. For the men it was a gala day, but for the women it was sadder than death. At 7.30 the long troop-train steamed out of the station, and having looked for the last time at the scenes of our battle rehearsals, we settled ourselves in our compartments, so excited with the consciousness of strife ahead that we could do nothing except smoke feverishly and laugh immoderately at each other's jokes. We stopped at none of the main stations of London, which on this genial Sunday night seemed to be drowsed in sleep. Twenty minutes after midnight we ran smoothly into Folkestone and detrained on the pier. Moored alongside was a fast transport, the *Onward,* belonging to the South-Eastern and

DISEMBARKATION

Chatham Railway, which swallowed us up in its black-hulled maw.

It was not yet dawn when the good ship slipped into the harbour of Boulogne, past the white lighthouses that are its sentinels. From the northern promontory a brilliant searchlight kept flashing across the Straits, dazzling white at its point of concentration, and gradually merging with the night as it broadened out in the distant waste of seas. Nothing escaped the sweep of that effulgent scimitar. A fishing smack came under the beam, and a barque lying in the roadstead, with its empty yards pointing to the stars, stood out boldly in that pool of illumination. The beam quivered for an instant, and then began to sweep over the restless waters. Farther south, outshone by this white brilliance, the lighthouse of Cap d'Alprech gleamed fitfully.

When the *Onward* was moored to the quay the order to disembark was shouted on the megaphone. There was no wild stampede ashore. On the contrary, the open spaces by the docks provided the opportunity for orderly formation. The battalion formed up in mass for the first time on French soil. Some fisherwomen were already abroad. They regarded the bare knees and bronzed faces with but careless appreciation. The populace was no longer *enthousiasmé*. The jubilant note of welcome was conspicuously wanting. No acclamations greeted us; no flowers fell in our path. We arrived when the good Boulonnais were asleep, and, save for a few strands of thin smoke curling slowly up from the military posts, there was nothing in the city to proclaim it one of the bases of our operations. When the town awoke we were no longer in its midst. A very tortuous and intolerably steep road took us to our resting-place, the camp of Ostrehove.

We had entertained hopes of a day's rest at Ostrehove, had flung ourselves down at haphazard in the tents that were provided for the comfort of reinforcements; but the altitude of the camp and its exposure to every keen wind that blew, added to the novelty of our being on a foreign soil, and that soil France, made rest impossible. The wind cut into our flesh like a knife. We tried to sleep, but only succeeded in dozing, heavy-eyed. Now and again, hearing the humming of aeroplanes, we would rush out to see them; or, unable to get the repose that tired nature should have exacted of us, we would wander over the heath and fill our lungs with those glorious breezes; and sometimes we were fain to plunge into stammering conversations with the chocolate sellers already come up from Boulogne to drive bargains with the Tommies. But we were destined to have no rest at Ostrehove. That at length seemed final. During breakfast, which we could hardly eat for excitement, the rumour spread that the battalion was to move early in the day. We crammed hard biscuits into our haversacks, and the tea, which we had swilled in our mess-tins, we drank to the lees. For this rumour was not an idle one. The order to move had arrived.

Before the sun had climbed high into the heavens we had left the shining uplands far behind us, and the dust from a thousand feet hung like a cloud over the tortuous road that twisted snakily into Pont de Briques. On the right, down below in the valley of the

Liane, two hospital trains, heavily laden, were crawling over the trunk line to Boulogne, so slowly that they seemed scarce to move. "The sight of those bandages," said my comrade many months after (he was himself killed at Beaumont-Hamel), " and the silent endurance on the faces of the sufferers made a greater impression on my mind than the sight of the dead lying in swathes."

On the march to Pont de Briques the inquisitive mind was constantly being stimulated by novel sights and sounds. Even the advertisements did not fail to attract interest. It is said that an ardent Scot, on arriving in France for the first time, was much impressed at finding a glorious advertisement for " Black and White." One could hear the men asking among themselves: " Byrrh ? Fat's ' Byrrh ' ? " The quaint shuttering of the windows always provoked merriment, and many a man saw there for the first time a sign that must be for ever engrained in his memory : " Chocolat Menier." At the station there were many odious comparisons between the amenities of French and Scottish railway stations. The northern mind could not appreciate the strange disc and chequer signals; and when the porter who was engaged in shunting operations drew from the pocket of his dirty blue culottes a melancholy horn, the laughter and derision knew no bounds.

At 9 a.m. a long train steamed into the station from the south. Hauled by an asthmatic omnibus locomotive, it jolted noisily past the platform. It was composed mainly of horse-boxes bedded with musty straw. Each wagon was designed to hold about forty men or eight horses *en long*.

We found that this train had come up from Havre with the advance party of the battalion. And now we understood how wide must be the organisation to arrange that this party which had left Bedford many days before us, and had gone by a much longer sea route, should rejoin the main body at a special rendezvous and at scheduled time. The question to which everybody was now keenly alive was our destination, and various theories were prompted by the embryo strategists of the battalion, not all of which bore the impress of probability. The officer who stated with a great show of dogmatic asseveration that we were going to the southern French front, was only induced to alter his opinion when on that well-known sickle of line just outside Calais the weary train shivered and stood still. Then for the first time grated on our ears the rude cries of dirty little children calling, "Beeskeets . . . geev beeskeets, Tom-mee . . . Bullee beef. . . ." Our interpreter, who had just been attached to us, chided them softly, and in the same breath shouted to their parents, who were regarding the whole affair with great unconcern, that we were going to the *fête*.

Shortly after midday the long discordant line of wagons began to crawl away from Calais, and, crossing the Rue de Guines, entered the region of the marshes and the canals. Flanders lay in front of us, the unhappy subject of all our hopes and fears and aspirations and disillusions. It was difficult to associate with all those boundless flats and intersecting threads of canals a history so poignant as was theirs. And yet on those very fields, so quiet and green, the spirit of age-old battles seemed to rest. A timorous and subdued people seemed to dwell upon them, recalling the time when in this red cockpit the furies of many nations swelled and were spent. There was much animated conversation on the subject of our journey, and a great deal of pointed criticism levelled at the railway officials and their methods of working. A budding optimist declared that the first station out of Calais, called Les Attaques, where we stopped as it seemed merely to gratify the whim of the stationmaster, was surely prophetic of our fortunes in the field. And indeed a passing study of the place-names *en route*, even by those whose etymological aptitude was not their most pronounced accomplishment, amply repaid any time devoted to it. Some appeared to be Scotch terms masquerading under a Flemish cloak, as in Nortkerke (Northkirk = Northchurch), or Steenstraete (Stanestreet = Stonestreet). Perhaps the most familiar feature of all these place-names, however, was the abundance of common suffixes, such as -ghem, -ecque, and -ouck.

As the history of the battalion is gradually unfolded in these pages, types of names embodying these peculiarities of termination will constantly be encountered.

At Hazebrouck, now a great centre of military activity, and sharing with St. Omer the distinction of being one of the main forward distributing foci, our train was diverted from the main line to a loop track of only secondary importance, although it fed the prosperous mining community that began at Béthune and centred at Lens. Men who had imposed on themselves the task of learning French, when they came to pronounce the names of this district must have felt that all their careful application had been in vain, for the euphony of the Gallic tongue was not to be found in names such as Morbecque, Steenbecque, or Molinghem. A few minutes after crossing the Aire Canal we jolted roughly into Berguette, a railway junction of some magnitude in these days when permanent ways and rolling stock formed such a valuable increment of the military capital. From Berguette a single branch line ran onwards to Merville, and finally rejoined the main track from Hazebrouck at Armentières.

The men were very tired, and their hunger was not to be appeased by the unpalatable fare which the necessities of a field campaign enforce. But strength was restored to the tired limbs by the roadside, and the little white-walled estaminet outside the village gave of its best—at a price—to those who had been prodigal of their resources or were reserving them for a more necessitous time. The day was genially hot; excessive marching had not yet blistered the feet; but, worn out by almost constant travelling under the most uncomfortable conditions, and parched by an unendurable thirst (we had yet to learn the importance of conserving the water supply), a march even of the merest distance was regarded as formidable. At the day's decline we fell in and marched to Cantrainne, a hamlet on the eastern fringe of Lillers, a distance of only six kilometres from our point of detrainment.

Most of the battalion was billeted in pleasant quarters on the road running parallel to the small river Nave. Where reeds did not spread too profusely, or where the muddy deposits were less objectionable, numbers of men plunged their bodies with unfeigned relish in its cold waters. Country maids tending the cattle were a natural check, till custom wore down their scruples almost to the point of invisibility. Battalion headquarters and my company (which at that time was " A ") found cover from the elements in the granaries of one Delalleau, a worthy and intelligent farmer who had not studied in vain from the most practical point of view the economics of agriculture. His novel methods, violating all the known canons of Highland farming, were an unceasing source of delight to the rural youth of Deeside, who gazed in open-mouthed amazement at a horse operating a threshing mill by means of a tread, or at a dog washing the good wife's linen by a modification of the same machine. The farmhouse itself was very old. M. Delalleau estimated its age at about four hundred years. And truly with its half-empty moat its appearance was venerable. The kitchen, province of two nimble-handed young women, who, by reason of the advancing senility and increasing deafness of *gran'mère*, were therefore her autocratic regents, was of those lofty dimensions which one instantly associates with the convivial splendours of generations long past. The spacious cellarage, butteries that must have had stored in their dimnesses casks filled with wine of the rarest bouquet, but now stored with homely *vin ordinaire* and cider, the huge baking ovens, the flagged floor excoriated with the feet of many generations surrounded this homestead with the glamour of mediaevalism. And when the deaf old woman hobbled over the stone *carrés* in her clumsy wooden sabots, the echoing stumble seemed to link one with the past.

Cantrainne being on the outskirts of Lillers, it was customary to pass the afternoons in the larger town. Here much of what was occurring in the forward theatre was reflected in the activities of the Motor Transport, whose personnel dropped hints of a coming offensive, which, though they were true in general, were nevertheless nebulous in detail. There was a clearing hospital here, and it was no uncommon sight to see wounded Indians arrive. We were infinitely struck with the proud, impassive faces, on which pain never seemed to make an impression. All these were visible evidences of the tragedy in which we were destined so soon to become actors. But there were other signs of the struggle. During the day it was possible to see just over the horizon little flecks of cloud that told of Archie. The guns we heard continually with varying intensity. Sometimes they sounded quite near, at other times they appeared to be far distant. Atmospheric changes accounted for the variability of sound. The noise of the guns was the clearest intimation that at last we were to partake of the glory of war, and some of us, too, knew that we would taste its bitterness. But the thought that some of the fine fellows, giants in frame and physique, would be as helpless as pygmies before those devouring guns, did not unduly disturb the serenity of our minds. At that moment everybody was imbued with an overmastering desire, to meet the enemy and put him to confusion.

For the space of a few days the battalion did very little except rest and await orders. The rest restored the strength of those who had found the initial hardships too exacting, and prepared them to endure the trials of coming days. On the 6th a route march was begun, but we had only reached the village of Busnettes when an urgent despatch recalled us hurriedly to billets. The rumour was whispered that we were to move up nearer to the line.

That this was no idle rumour was confirmed at a consultation between the Colonel and his officers. At 6 p.m. the battalion resumed its march forward. All were agreed that it was one of the most villainous marches it had ever been our misfortune to experience. Unaccustomed to the deceptive similarity of the country and the wayside landscapes, particularly at night, it was indeed difficult to avoid losing direction. And as this was of the nature of a forced march, the difficulties were increased tenfold. The stragglers had to be harried to keep up with the column. So unequal was the pace that every few minutes the battalion was alternately rushing forward and slowing down. Little wonder that, almost overcome by the excessive task that had been set, the troops tottered into Quentin and slept where they fell, some not even throwing off their equipment. In this night march it fell to my lot to collect a note of the billets vacated so hurriedly, whereby I was considerably delayed. The supply of maps had not at this time reached the high state of excellence that characterised the operations of a later date. I had no more information than that the battalion had gone somewhere " near Paradis." And with these vague instructions I had to rest content. Maps not having been issued, at least to the subordinate officers, I was compelled to find my way by the interrogation of civilians. In Busnes my small party was held up for a time by a dreadful congestion of transport. The crossroads were blocked by every species of vehicle. The Brigade-Major, with all the skill at his command, did succeed in restoring order and releasing the held-up traffic. At Busnes, when the congestion was most pronounced, I met Ross bringing up the rear guard. His men had become hopelessly interlocked in the mass of wagons, and, when the march was resumed, there was no longer any touch kept with the main body. The terrible monotony of Flanders, especially when the impenetrable heat mists rolled fold on fold over the ground, made even the shortest march seem long and uncomfortable. And this blind struggle to a destination of which we confessed we had but the haziest notions, was as trying to the body as it was distressing to the mind. How inexpressibly thankful we were when, almost in despair of finding a solution to all our difficulties, we heard the well-known voice of Kennington, and saw, looming through the morning mist, the wagons unloading the baggage and the cookers preparing for the early meal.

Worn out by fatigue I threw myself down in the first barn I saw, and slept so soundly that not even the rats crawling over my body could make me stir. Many a time after I envied myself the serenity of that sleep.

Next morning a billet was found for the

officers of my company in the outhouse of the Estaminet de la Rue Dubois, wherein we supped a great many times, for the good woman had not an equal in the art of making omelettes, and head-quarters, a few doors distant, were in the humour to envy us our good fortune. At the coming round of evening the young country peasants used to enter, and, sitting down, call in their gruff patois for coffee, for which they tendered a few sous. Then they would charge their pipes so fully that the vile French tobacco stood an inch above the rim, and light the weed at the venthole of the range and smoke in silence. These peasants were in sober contrast to the chattering females, of whom they did not dare to fall foul, but, grumbling audibly about the prices of things, would begrudge even the small perforated Belgian coin and steal away into the night. Madame, being keeper of the purse, knew the economics of the house better than any one. And in her transactions over the counter promises to pay were of no avail. "Quand ce coq chantera," read the picture, "on fera crédit." And it was on these profitable lines of business that most of the estaminets were run. This print was usually flanked on one side by a representation of all the principal currencies of the world, and on the other by a law published against *Ivresse.*

Meanwhile, the hints let fall at Lillers were now being realised as a certainty. The preparations for the big attack projected on the front of Aubers were in course of development. For a week preceding the battle the most sanguine hopes were entertained of complete success. The French were said to be co-operating on the right to seize the commanding ground held by the enemy in the region of Neuville St. Vaast. Whether our push was to be of the nature of a demonstration or not could not be determined. But that the plans for the attack had already been formulated, and were soon to be carried into effect, were facts too obvious to be ignored. On the night of the 8th the Colonel consulted with his officers. Confirming orders had arrived. At 4 o'clock next morning the preliminary bombardment was to take place, of great intensity, immediately after which the German trenches in the vicinity of Neuve Chapelle were to be carried by assault. We were to be prepared to move at a moment's notice, as any unforeseen success beyond that which was anticipated might involve us in an action of movement on the heels of a retreating enemy. But the disastrous enterprise of May 9th, shattered at its very inception, found us still in Quentin awaiting the order that never came.

At 4 o'clock we were awakened by the roll of the artillery. Instant preparations were made for departure. Blankets were rolled up; officers' valises were stacked ready for transport; the morning meal was got ready hastily; but the minutes passed by, and ugly rumours began to circulate. Had the attack broken down? Or, in contradiction to these rumours, had we carried our objectives after all? Those who were supposed to know shook their heads wisely, but would communicate no news. We saw a troop of Bengal Lancers ride furiously up, and detected therein omens of victory. Surely, we said in our ignorance, these men are going up to chase the defeated Huns. But still the welcome order to advance did not reach us. At 11.45 a.m. the artillery duel, which had moderated in the interim, became more intense, but its violence was not prolonged, and soon disappeared altogether.

Meanwhile the duties demanded of us at Quentin were not arduous. The rest freshened up the men, but the billets were miserably poor. On the night of our arrival some confusion arose through the men stumbling in upon the privacy of the inhabitants. Captain Adam had a triangled contest with an old woman and her pig. This epic will live for ever in the history of the battalion. At two in the morning the animal was routed out of its sty, and its vigorous protestations, in the form of sundry grunts and squeals, caused such a clamour that the decrepit owner hobbled out into the courtyard and added to the general outcry. In the darkness pig and men dashed into each other, and in the din the old woman's voice shrilled out in breathless monosyllables: " Le cochon! Le cochon! Dis . . . pa . . . ru." On the

7th Mulvey and myself journeyed to Merville, an attractive town whose acquaintance we were destined to form at a later period. In those days of our innocence it was customary for us to call such a simple journey as this by the grandiose title of "road reconnaissance." At the fork roads from Pacaut to Paradis there is a quaint little estaminet, and here we refreshed our thirst with a new beverage, Sirop de Grenadines, for which we paid the sum of two centimes per glass. On another day I motored into Calonne-sur-la-Lys to requisition wood, potatoes, and coal. Although nominally on the River Lys, this town is actually on the twin rivers (or courants) of Clarence and Noc. Calonne is notable only for the ruins of an old church, whose antecedents I had neither the opportunity nor the inclination to investigate.

The failure of the attack on Aubers Ridge seemed for the moment to dislocate our programme. On the 12th we returned to those very billets at Cantrainne which we had vacated so hastily on the evening of the 6th. But this was neither a forced nor a night march. We accomplished it at our leisure, passing through the town of Robecq, which was then thronged with Indians. The battalion remained at Cantrainne for the space of two days and then marched to Caestre, at a distance of over thirty kilometres. The roads were all constructed of hard *pavés*, which blistered our feet and fatigued us long before the pleasant rolling lands of Caestre showed on the horizon. But the route was full of interest, and the transition from the Pas de Calais to the Nord Department proved so fruitful of enjoyment that our minds were kept from flagging and our feet from failing. We crossed three large and important canals, the Aire, Lys, and Nieppe. The latter derived its name from the forest of the district, through which runs a perfectly straight road between the villages of Haverskerque and Steenbecque. In this forest large gangs of Frenchmen were hard at work felling trees and sawing planks for trench *matériel*. The towns of St. Venant and Hazebrouck, too, flocked to their doors to see a brigade wholly attired in the *petit jupon*.

The map position of Caestre once more

directed our minds to the vexed question of our ultimate destination. When we were at Lillers it was thought not unlikely that we would take over on the front somewhere between La Bassée and Neuve Chapelle, and our subsequent move to Quentin heightened that likelihood almost into certainty. But here we now found ourselves at a town which was on the direct line to Poperinghe and Ypres. What thought more natural than that we should soon be in the trenches of the Salient? Yet, strange to say, from the time of its arrival in France till that eventful month of November 1916, when I had the misfortune to be severely wounded, my division spent not so much as an hour in that desolated abattoir.

It will not readily be forgotten by some of the original battalion how, in the circumscribed amphitheatre of a Flemish farmyard wherein was all manner of divers smells, an appreciative audience, with whom the Major himself did not feel it undignified to be in collusion, assembled one afternoon to witness the sportiveness of a pig. The mists of the past cloud the memory; the figures loom up strange and indefinable like the figures seen through a fog; but the merry wrinkle of laughter still creeps round the eyes when that historic occasion is recalled. Alas! How many can recall it?

On the 17th we quitted Caestre for Neuf Berquin, about ten kilometres farther ahead, finding it a low-lying place full of sombre houses and miserable hovels. Traces of guerrilla fighting were everywhere evident in Neuf Berquin. A great many of the walls bore the marks of bullets, and in the house where I chanced to be billeted the Germans had put up a stout resistance by knocking a hole in the wall and keeping the French at bay with a machine-gun. The two old people in the house were deplorably reduced. They made us warm coffee when we took possession, but we did not discover at the time that they had neither money nor food in the house sufficient to keep life in their bodies. We gave ham and cheese to the woman, and the man went into raptures over a liberal supply of English tobacco. But we had no time to cultivate further the acquaintance of these two interesting people, for next evening another forward movement brought us to Pont Riqueult near Lestrem. We left Neuf Berquin shortly after 8 o'clock, but an unfortunate contretemps arose which forced us to halt on the *pavé* just outside the village, and remain there under a bitter wind and a drizzle from which we could obtain no respite. Some of the men actually fell asleep on the metals. Several fainted from the extreme cold. At 12.45 the march was resumed, and three hours later, so weary that our limbs almost refused to answer our wills, we trudged slowly into Pont Riqueult. Here the mud was ankle-deep everywhere, but we were so sleepy and fatigued that we did not stay even to scrape our boots, but lay down and knew no more.

Gradually we were approaching the firing line. At each successive stage the war took on a fresher significance. The noise of the guns, which we had heard only indistinctly at Lillers, and more definably at Caestre, here met our ears as a deep and defiant roar. The flecks of smoke which the good people of Cantrainne had forbodingly pointed out on the far horizon, were now almost directly overhead. The star shells shone with increasing brilliance. And the division had suffered its first casualties.

| II | TOMMY AND HIS TRENCH |

AN apology is required to explain the introduction at this early stage of a somewhat didactic chapter. While it is regretted that the natural connection of the narrative is impaired, it is nevertheless hoped that it will be found useful in throwing light upon many terms to be employed in succeeding chapters whose meaning would otherwise remain obscure. To any soldier this chapter will convey nothing new, and can most conveniently be skipped. It is primarily intended for those who have never had the advantage of military training or seen service overseas.

War teaches war. Each successive campaign sheds fresh light on the most horrible science in the world. Every campaign, every engagement, whether it be decisive or not, influences its successor. The trenches of the academies, book-learnt, the trenches of the manœuvre ground, manned when not a shot is fired in anger, all are subject to alteration when the enemy is within gunshot. The superior power of an army allows it to impose its will upon the weaker adversary. It has the advantage of being able to select the most favourable trench position, while the enemy has to content himself with a very indifferent terrain. It is this adjustment of position to local conditions of ground, this continual revolt from the domination of a superior position, that explain the endless variety of trenches to be described in this book. No two sectors are quite alike. But there are certain elements of static warfare common to all areas. The general outlines, while they must conform to the conditions imposed either by the enemy, or by the nature of the ground in dispute, are as unalterable as the very constructional details of the trenches themselves. It will be my intention in this chapter to set forth those common elements.

It is necessary from the outset to confine the attention to the first-line system, because in the case of the second-line a freer selection in the siting permits the uniform use of the most favourable ground, and in this respect the differences can never be so apparent. There can only be inherent differences, such as are occasioned by the general slope, the direction and height of the ridges, and so forth. From the second-line, too, must be eliminated the idea of immediate conformity to enemy pressure. Popular imagination has seized upon these very indefinite terms, and in giving them birth in utterance has limited their meanings far within the actual interpretation. To a large number of men the common phrase "first-line" conveys the impression of the foremost trench on the front, and the foremost trench alone. "Second-line" is usually held to be a synonym of the support trench, and, correspondingly, "third-line" is often applied to the reserve trench. But the "first-line" is an inclusive term for the firing line, the support trench, and the reserve trench. The "first-line" is the system, complete in trench appointment, confronting the enemy. The "second-line" may be one or two or even three miles to the rear, and is usually incomplete, while the "third-line" is more often merely a line on paper, ready to be transformed, it is true, into a defensive position if retirement upon it is rendered necessary, but still—on paper.

Trench fighting may be considered as only a phase of the grander operations of war. And the trenches themselves, at most, can only pretend to be the scene of negative, as apart from positive or active warfare—warfare of movement. In structure and general trace they are not reducible to any recognised rule, because they are so wholly dependent on the ever-fluctuating conditions of time and place. What determines their structure are the prevailing nature of the ground, its height above sea level, its height relative to contiguous features, its power of domination over other parts in enemy occupation, or, *vice versa*, its own exposure to enemy domination. Thus our trenches at the Quinque Rue, before Festubert, my personal knowledge of which dates to June 1915, and at Houplines, immediately to the right of the Lys, were in reality breastworks, actual excavation being rendered impossible on account of the nearness of the water level to the surface of the ground. Opposite Bécourt, to take an example from the Somme, the trenches were shallow rather than deep; but reverting to the north, we find that Douai Avenue, in the Labyrinth overlooked by the German trenches of Thélus, was dug down to a depth of over nine feet.

As regards the general trace the achievements of men are the great conditioning factors, always subject of course to the various natural features. Where human prowess has given to our arm the choice of position, we have been able to site our trenches where they can be most effectively offensive. In those places where, owing to numerical inferiority, we have been unable to claim that inestimable advantage, the poor alternative has faced us of suiting an inferior position to meet our defensive rather than our offensive needs. The variable fortunes of trench warfare render it certain that an unbroken continuity of favourable positions can with difficulty be realised. Before any widely organised offensive, however, that must be the primary object, clearly defined

TOMMY AND HIS TRENCH

in theory and resolutely aimed at in practice. And by a proper understanding of this fact all those numberless " minor engagements," doomed too often to inglorious obscurity, acquire a new importance and are seen to be indissolubly linked with all the dashing advances which a sudden and sustained publicity thrusts upon the world. This constant change, whether it be by the convulsive upheaval of a general offensive or by the activity of local encounters, whether it be the hard-won advancement of our line or the irruption and break-down of our defences, can, in general survey, be made to explain the series of salients and re-entrants stretching from the sea to Switzerland.

Tactically considered, the whole trench system is divided into " fronts," or, in the case of armies, army corps, or divisions, where the sphere of control recedes much farther, it is found convenient to speak of " areas." One hears tell, for instance, of the " front of the 15th Army Corps," or the " 3rd Army Area." Or again, translating into actualities, the 3rd Army may, so to speak, hold the front from the La Bassée

Canal to the River Lys. The 15th Army Corps Area may comprise for the purposes of its jurisdiction all the ground whose outermost limits are marked by the towns of Lens, Gommecourt, Doullens, and Frévent. These large partitions are divided into sectors and sub-divided into sub-sectors. A sector is commonly allotted to a brigade, and it is the general rule to find three sub-sectors forming the brigade front. Each sub-sector is a trench system complete in itself, but complementary to its neighbours. Its integrity and upkeep are entrusted to the battalion whose commander is responsible for its defence, and must hand it over to any incoming unit on the completion of his period of guardianship, preferably stronger, but at all costs as intact as when he assumed control.

The length of a sub-sector varies continually with the degree of opposition manifested by the enemy, with the delicacy of the operations necessary for its proper defence, and with the number of the troops available to man its fire-steps. The sub-sector is in reality a triple belt of trenches, all in perfect communication and supported as frequently as the ground permits by subordinate lines and intermediate strong points. The salient features (how commonplace do these terms sound!) are the "firing line," the "support trench," and the "reserve trench"; but there may be in addition a carefully blinded secondary support trench (as before Beaumont-Hamel), and in exceptional cases (as in the Labyrinth) the development of an observation line in front of all. The evolution of this particular type of trench will in a later chapter be treated in some detail. Furthermore may be found what are called "assembly trenches," where men are massed prior to an attack. Differentiation of type is constantly encountered, and there is always an inclination to modify the existing system by the addition of subsidiary lines.

Intercommunication is everywhere maintained by an extensive network of sub-level passages, except where the dead nature of the ground permits traffic without the necessity of artificial protection. Besides the ordinary communication trenches, there are several other channels of moving men and supplies from one point to another in comparative safety. It is a common feature, for instance, to witness line upon line of trench tramways leading to the very foremost position. What a boon these tramways are to the men, who would otherwise be compelled to carry heavy loads of provisions, shells for the trench mortars, small arms ammunition, can readily be imagined. Farther to the rear these tramways give way to light railways feeding the batteries, which in their turn are displaced by the ordinary track, upon which runs a very fine service of military trains worked by the Railway Operating Division. These main lines run back as far as the base. But there remains a third type of trench, which instead of communicating from front to rear is yet a traffic trench and auxiliary to the main line. Its function is to provide as ready an access as possible between one point of the firing line and another. It runs parallel to it, but is not traversed.

This vital distinction brings us to a consideration of the constructional details of

TOMMY AND HIS TRENCH

the trenches themselves, a subject so wide and technical that a mere enumeration only is possible within the limits of this book. The front line and, indeed, all fire trenches are irregularly traced. When they are subject to a definite irregularity they are said to be traversed. No continuously straight line could withstand the dangers of oblique and enfilade fire. A fire trench is divided into traverses and bays, the latter being about ten yards in length, and fire-stepped to accommodate six men. The parapet, to be satisfactory, must be bullet-proof, a condition much more essential where the trenches are of the nature of breastworks. A suitable parados, too, must be provided to guard against back-blast. The sides must be revetted by expanded metal, interwoven branches, or gabions, a device affected by the French and much discredited. Provision has to be made for trench stores, local ammunition dumps, bomb receptacles, gas alarm posts, dug-outs, overhead protection for sentries, sally ports, and a thousand different items. Sanitary measures are of vital necessity. Latrines have to be numerous and scientifically constructed. Drainage by sump holes or natural flowing off demands constant and unwearying attention.

A battalion's dominion, when it is in occupation of a particular sector, is restricted to the scene where it plays all its multifarious parts of activity—the cold, muddy, death-ridden trenches themselves—and those earthy dungeons where it seeks a momentary repose. The constituents of an ordinary trench have been laid down in the preceding paragraphs. But to the lay mind the construction of a dug-out is an affair that presents bewildering difficulties. Generally speaking, we may trace the development of what is now recognised as a dug-out from the spring of 1915. Previous to that date the thinly held and meagre extent of line occupied by our troops was totally unsuitable for deep excavation. Shelter from the elements alone by means of sand-bagged chambers, or mere holes scooped out of the parapet, made provision for the rest that was so necessary to reinvigorate them. Such shelter was wholly inadequate to protect them from the dangers of shell fire.

TOMMY AND HIS TRENCH

Gradually, however, as the months advanced and reinforcements of territorial regiments poured out to relieve the jaded first divisions, we were able to extend our line southwards, taking over from the French and elsewhere stiffening our own emaciated brigades. A complete change of soil was now apparent. The more removed we were from Flanders the more able we were to dig down without flooding the trenches with a superabundance of water. And as the enemy's artillery showed promise of growing heavier and still heavier, there was a continued incentive to hard and unremitting labour. There could be no standardisation of dug-outs, however, on account of ever-varying conditions, but at the opening of the Somme offensive in July 1916, a depth of less than fourteen feet was considered by our meticulous foe as being dangerous and untenable.

The scientific construction of a dug-out has been decided upon only after very severe and exacting tests. It must not be imagined that to sink an oblique and stepped shaft to a chamber fulfilling the depth condition just stated, and merely to have it timbered and propped, is a guarantee of complete immunity from disaster. An 8-inch percussion and delayed-action shell, scoring a direct hit, would very effectually seal the fate of any occupants of such a tottering death trap. The genius of the Royal Engineers has been applied to the task of determining what thickness of roof is consistent with the integrity of the dug-out and the safety of the men. And the constituents of the roof provide a most entertaining and profitable study. The German manual *Stellungsbau*, dated June 1916, immediately preceding the battle of the Somme, estimated that a roof of 14·75 feet, if properly constructed, was for ordinary purposes sufficiently shell-proof.

Let us now consider what particular elements rendered it shell-proof. The dug-out itself was propped with heavy logs, and the walls, if they were not entirely planked, were at least provided with an adequate skirting board. The value of this item, in conjunction with a boarded or concreted floor, will at once be appreciated when one considers the hordes of rats that infested these places, the damps that made bare, earthy walls chilly to touch and view, and, conversely, the cheerful comfort of places made bright with pictures of home—"Kirchnerised," if one may coin the expression. A stout layer of timber baulks formed the inner roof, resting upon vertical props. A cushion of 1·6 feet of earth separated these from a double layer of logs, intended to give the whole an elastic resiliency were it to suffer the shock of a bursting shell. A further cushion of earth, 3·8 feet in thickness, supervened between this and another arresting course, composed of a duplicated layer of fascines, laid crossways, four fascines thick. Another earth cushion of 2·7 feet, and lastly a stratum of stones. This was technically known as a bursting course, intended to detonate any shell if enemy marksmanship should happen to be accurate, or fortuitous enough to register a direct hit. Such is a typical example of dug-out then in vogue; but it must be distinctly understood that the selection of a particular pattern is entirely dependent upon the conditions of the ground that govern the digging capabilities of the troops, and the degree of artillery hostility that forces them to burrow like moles deeper and deeper into the earth.

So far we have considered only the trenches involved and the tenements that form an integral part of them. Let us now turn briefly to the human material, its dispositions, its duties—routine and otherwise—its specialist personnel, and so forth. On paper a battalion establishment is one thousand and odd men. But he who imagines that a unit can count on such a rifle strength is greatly deceived. One must look not for the rifle strength that appears on paper, but for the net rifle strength, the number of men actually available to take a combatant part in any operation, whether it be to repel a sudden assault or to *acheminer* an offensive. A battalion is fortunate, indeed, if it is capable of mustering 600 for such services. Ordinarily speaking it is necessary to deduct cooks, transport men, R.A.M.C. orderlies and stretcher-bearers, quartermaster's stores, men reported sick or otherwise unfit for duty, men on leave, men on courses and detached duties, and during the progress of a push a certain

TOMMY AND HIS TRENCH

proportion of officers, non-commissioned officers, and specialists temporarily withheld to replace if need be casualties sustained in their respective ranks.

As a general rule the battalion puts three companies into the front lines and retains the fourth as supports. The distribution of duties varies. It may be, as was the case in the Labyrinth, that it is inadvisable for tactical reasons to detach men from the front line for the purpose of conveying rations to their comrades. This has to be performed by fatigue parties drawn from the supports. The men in the front line, however, have usually to supply such fatigues as are found necessary to conserve the integrity of their trenches. They have, besides, to furnish sentry groups, varying in number by day and night, and have to man observation posts and undertake any perilous enterprise, such as patrols, as the exigencies of the situation demand.

The particular offices of the specialists, on the other hand, absolve them, except in the case of bombers, from such free employment. Time was, however, when the bombers, exulting in a terrible monopoly of hand grenades and drain-pipes, a highly specialised and exclusive minority, were totally exempt from the necessity of submitting themselves to the common duty of sentry-go. Now they are not so privileged, for the simple reason that every man in the battalion must have graduated through the bombing schools and become an expert and licensed anarchist. As regards bombs and bomb-stores, each company officer is responsible for the upkeep of all establishments in his platoon area. The company commander is likewise responsible to his commanding officer that there is an adequate supply of these redoubtable weapons available for instant use. General supervision is exercised by an officer specially detailed for this important duty, and upon him rests the onus of instructing the men in the principles of grenade fighting.

Machine gunners figure largely in the economy of trench protection. They may belong either to the Machine Gun Corps, or may be part of the battalion personnel specialised in the use of the machine gun. Both bodies are represented in every battalion sector. A different type of weapon is employed by each. In the former the improved Vickers Gun is used. But with the latter the much more easily assembled Lewis Gun finds especial favour. Machine gun emplacements, when well constructed, command unstinted admiration. When carelessly made they are a constant source of danger and annoyance on account of the large amount of unnecessary fire that they draw upon us. They may be either open or covered. Considering each case, open emplacements are found to be a tray or concrete platform let into the parapet. They are used only during the hours of darkness or when in the case of an attack their suitability of meeting it determines their employment. Covered emplacements, on the other hand, are strongly protected and very skilfully disguised. The conditioning factors determining their site are a good field of fire, concealment from direct observation, and accessibility.

A great deal of attention, well merited as it is, has been directed to the machine gunners to the detriment of the other sections of specialist. For instance, the intelligence branch performs a work which for actual value probably exceeds all others. Its daily report records all information, and even trivial things which would escape the attention of the untrained eye are found to be of incalculable value. The watchful eye of the scout must be for ever gleaning scraps of information, which, when collated, provide material from which inferences of great import may be drawn. Normally the Intelligence Section numbers among its personnel the snipers. Heedless of weather conditions, collected in danger, and nerved to endure the ordeal of patiently waiting a favourable opportunity in a post none too safe, must describe these men. Quickness of perception is a very necessary attribute of theirs. They must be thoroughly trained in shooting at moving and swiftly vanishing objects. Their eyesight must be acute enough to distinguish the head of an enemy slowly appearing over the parapet or passing a danger spot. They must be able to judge distance at a moment's notice, although a good scout will have worked out a schedule of distance tables beforehand. They must be proficient in the use of optical sights, field glasses, and periscopes. They must possess the perceptions of the artist in assimilating their camouflaging colours to their surroundings. They must be capable of appreciating the advantages of artificial cover. Immobility, silence, and an infinite patience they must possess. Map-reading should have no terrors for them, and the art of drawing up a concise report should be a part of their manifold resources.

These paragraphs do not exhaust the manifold operations of the specialist sections. Signals, on whose meticulous accuracy in the transmission of messages, on whose coolness and daring when the wires are broken, largely depends the success of attack or defence, would engross a volume to themselves for the proper explication of their services.

III   THE FIRST SHOT

ON the 20th a further step forward was made when we bivouacked in a field adjoining the Calvary of Mesplaux. This rectangular plot of ground was about a mile south-east of Locon, and not far distant from the Lawe Canal. Here the troops prepared themselves for the coming ordeal. The rations were carefully examined; defective field dressings were replaced; the question of taking over was gone into as thoroughly as possible in the circumstances. The men were drilled in fire-control by those who had seen active service elsewhere, and who knew the value of being sparing of ammunition. At night the sky was full of strange flashes and the tat-tat . . . tat-tat-tat of machine guns broke in upon the silence. Although these two days were spent in idle anticipation, the thrill of approaching battle was everywhere manifest. Nowhere was this

THE FIRST SHOT

more so than in the letters which we were unwillingly forced to censor. A spirit so admirable could not fail to produce the finest results.

Meanwhile the 5th Gordons had taken over trenches from the Canadians in the sector of Richebourg. On the 22nd an alarm was given, and we were aroused from our sleep to move up towards the trenches. The night was brilliant with star-shells and gun-flashes, and there was such a crescendo of noise that, although I have heard it eclipsed hundreds of times since then, till that moment I had never hearkened to a more intense volume. The alarm was false, and at Le Touret we turned and retraced our steps.

On the following evening the 5th Gordons were due for relief. At 7 p.m., the night being calm and clear, we paraded and marched off, splitting up into platoons when the Rue du Bois was reached, in order to lessen the danger of casualties. At the reserve trench, guides, who since their baptism of fire were inclined to treat us with heavy facetiousness, were placed in readiness. It was pitch-dark when the relief was completed. The

THE FIRST SHOT

ghostly queues finally settled down at their appointed stations. But the trenches were so execrably planned that much valuable time was lost in the operation. In the first instance there was only one communication trench, and it was too narrow for the passage of two men abreast. The 5th Gordons, therefore, had to lie behind the parados until the front trench was fully manned. To add to our difficulties, these lines had been captured from the enemy but a few days previously, and the fire-steps all faced the wrong way. There was not a scrap of wire in front. The Germans, however, if this was any consolation to our minds, were not properly dug in. Opposing us at this part were the 56th and 57th Westphalian Regiments and the 15th Jager Regiment. The battalion was disposed with "A" and "B" companies in the front line, "C" in support, and "D" in reserve. We had but two machine guns posted on either flank!

We were in our places by 1 a.m. The whine of a shell came down to us on the wind. Flares from the enemy, bathing the earth in a cold, white glare, disclosed little.

THE FIRST SHOT

Mounds looked like men, and distant avenues of trees like massed battalions. Fears too fantastic to be real assailed the faint of heart. Our nerves, strung to the highest pitch, kept us constantly peering over the parapet. Our ignorance was phenomenal. We did not know at what distance lay the enemy. Some were unaware even of the enemy's direction! We longed for dawn to come. About 2 a.m., above the sullen roar of the guns, pealed a terrific blast of thunder. The lightning flashed down the bayonets with a weird effect. As it was dawning a little more could be distinguished—an open field of fire of about 600 yards, torn up by shells, and a frontage of ruins. A group of trees on the left, sadly shattered and stripped of their branches and leaves, alone mitigated the loneliness of these waste places. The dead lay thick in front. Five were huddled up not more than twelve yards away from me. They were Coldstreamers. Several Indians, too, were lying there, but their features were almost unrecognisable. We spent that first morning repairing the trenches and making them more habitable,

THE FIRST SHOT

As day advanced we became more and more accustomed to our surroundings. Our neighbours on either flank were the 5th Seaforths and the 7th Black Watch. They, too, had experienced the same initial difficulties. We *were* tyros in those days. Whenever we heard a shell approaching we jumped up to see it burst. Appreciative or deprecating remarks greeted each missile. "That was a good one!" . . . "Bad shot, Fritz, try again!" . . . and so on, *usque ad nauseam*. In the evening we detected the enemy bringing up, or clandestinely trying to remove, a field gun. We opened fire with a machine gun on the right flank and accounted for some of the detachment, but not before they had time to slew it round and fire on the trench at point-blank range. I shall never forget that sheet of red death. That night, too, there was some more liveliness manifested along the line. Once or twice the rumour spread that the Germans were attacking, rumours entirely without foundation. At one time, when the reports multiplied thick and fast and reached the support trench in such a garbled state that

THE FIRST SHOT

it was believed that the front line had fallen, "Come on, lads!" shouted a captain; "who'll follow me?" and straightway sprang over the parapet. But the front line was perfectly entire, and the enemy were in possession of no trench elements.

The initiation of the Division was a very severe test, inasmuch as we did not graduate through the hands of experienced instructors, but, unacclimatised to trench conditions, had to hold ground that was dangerous to a degree. In point of fact our first taste of war was that supervening process of a successful attack—consolidation. It was perhaps fortunate that we did not fully appreciate the extreme gravity of such a situation. Nowadays consolidation is regarded as being as important as the actual assault, and fraught with an equal if not greater danger. What do we mean by the term "consolidation"? We mean, in brief, the substitution of a defensive British for a captured German position. As soon as the hostile trenches are carried, they have to be reversed in their employment. What once was parados must now become parapet, and *vice versa.* The whole system has to be re-fire-stepped to meet the new requirements. Wire must be strung along the new front. The trenches must have suffered during our bombardment, and they need constant repair. And, above all, the troops must be doubly vigilant in order to prevent the debouching of a counter-attack or frustrate it if it gathers weight.

On the 25th we were taken out of the line, being relieved by the King's Liverpool Regiment of the 154th Brigade. During this time we lost in casualties a total of twenty-five men, of whom two died of their wounds. These casualties had a tendency to increase as the days advanced, because the enemy's guns, having at last been ranged on the lost positions, became daily more aggressive. Relief, however, which began on the evening of the 25th, was not completed till an early hour of the following day; and so overcome were we by sleep and fatigue that the effort of walking back was almost mechanical. With nodding heads and half-shut eyes we toiled back to billets. For a few hours we shared along

THE FIRST SHOT

with Strathcona's Horse the lodgment of a large empty house on the banks of the Lawe Canal. These same Canadians had been on our immediate right, and in the course of a minor action had lost considerably. But the survivors, keen and eager to revenge their fallen comrades, thirsted again for that mad moment when the lust of killing surges to the brain. As the day wore on the men relaxed themselves and restored their vigour, first by much-needed sleep and then by a plunge in the cool waters of the canal. But it became evident that an alteration of the billeting arrangements was imperative, for another squadron of Canadians arrived, and we were improperly quartered in their area. The transference of the whole company, therefore, took place that night to the quiet little village of Pont d'Avelette, situate between Chocques and Hinges and astride the Aire Canal. "D" Company signalised its arrival in this village by the arrest of two suspected spies, found hiding in a barn. They were removed under strong escort for examination, but what their ultimate fate was I am unable to say.

THE FIRST SHOT

We had left the shores of England under the impression, common to all fresh troops, that nothing was a-wanting in our military education. We prided ourselves on the most expert knowledge of the technique of war. Musketry could no longer terrify, field operations could yield up no more secrets. We had attained the *ne plus ultra* of the most dreadful science in the world. Such was our belief, and nothing could shake it. But there was one little branch, hitherto neglected, soon to enforce its striking claims and shatter our vain dreams of omniscience. And that branch was—Bombing. True, a beginning had been made at Bedford, when it became recognised that the bomb was not the mere discredited weapon of the anarchist, but a potentiality capable of influencing tactics and modifying operations. But the beginning was a feeble effort, and lack of material almost strangled it. Now and henceforward steps had to be taken to correct that omission, in order that, with the new principles of trench warfare applied, the fighting value of the unit might be immeasurably increased. A bomb school,

THE FIRST SHOT

therefore, was formed and suitable instructors appointed. A lecture ground was chosen at a farmhouse situated centrally between Lacouture and Richebourg St. Vaast. Of these two villages the former was extensively damaged and almost devoid of inhabitants. Strange to say at this time the church alone seemed to be immune from the effects of shell fire. But if Lacouture made us sorrowful, Richebourg should have drawn tears to our eyes, for the hand of the destroyer lay heavy upon it. It was a famous desolation. The marks of shrapnel were apparent on every house. I entered one which seemed to have been vacated hurriedly. There was still a chromo-lithograph of the late Pope hanging on the wall. It was mildewy, for the rains blew in and two gaping holes showed in the roof. There was a baby's cradle in the corner, overturned. On putting it upright I found some of the infant's apparel. Where is the woman who sang her *berceuse* in those happy days before the war? And then the church! Woodwork in matchwood, the tower scattered among uprooted graves, the whole edifice split

THE FIRST SHOT

in two pieces almost falling asunder. The sight of all these things made us turn aside with a grievous heart. If the unfortunate country had suffered all this sad mischance legitimately at the hands of an enemy past master in the art of waging ruthless war, much would have been forgiven.

Our billet was comfortable, but crowded, in the house of an excellently disposed woman, who used to provide us with sweet omelettes and vile beer. Her beer we discontinued when it was found that a small cask could be obtained without much difficulty from Béthune. The officers at the bomb school were drawn from the four battalions of my Brigade (153rd), and we had many interests in common. One I had known as an ardent cadet in Edinburgh University Officers' Training Corps. He was posted as missing after the explosion of a German mine in the Labyrinth in the late spring of 1916. Another we knew as the pessimist of the school. He was always foretelling evil, but in a genial humorous way that made us burst out laughing. He was killed instantaneously some three weeks

A RUINED FARMHOUSE NEAR RICHE-
BOURG

THE FIRST SHOT

later by a shell at the notorious "L 8" of Festubert. A third we took to be a quiet and unassuming chap until one night there was a farmyard concert about 1 a.m. And then he used an extensive and *recherché* vocabulary. He was very severely wounded a few weeks afterwards at Festubert. Another was the very essence of good humour. We used to read to him extracts from *John Bull* when that paper was handling his distinguished relative rather roughly. He received a mortal wound shortly after.

There were no hours that sped so light-winged as these. It was a gay and irresponsible mess. No thought of approaching dissolution came to darken our horizons. And yet within what a short space of time was death to make his inexorable inroads! Paddy, a miner from Fifeshire, was the life and soul of us. Without speaking a single word of French he could twist Madame round his little finger, make her produce eggs, omelettes, milk, beer, and cooking utensils by the most marvellous legerdemain in the world. When we called Paddy he would

THE FIRST SHOT

enter, the corner of his eyes furrowing with ill-suppressed mirth.

" Sirr ! "

" Ask Madame for some milk, Paddy. The rice pudding you've made is like a desert."

" Mulk . . . bit she'll no' un'erstan', sirr."

" Oh, show her the cow, Paddy ! Say *du lait*; say anything you like, but get the milk."

" Doo lay ? Ye mane coo lay. . . . Madame, coo lay, ye ken, the lay o' the coo . . . no' compree ? "

Paddy goes through the motion of milking a cow. Madame, comprehendingly, " O mais wêh, monsieur . . . lait, pour des officiers, hein ? "

Or again :

" Paddy, get a coffee-pot."

" Madame, coffee-pot." More melodramatic gestures, as a result of which Madame brings forth a small jug. Paddy surveys it with a distraught air, and bursts out :

" Hoots, wumman, it winna haud eneuch co-fee t'slocken the cat's thrapple. Gie's anither. A bigger yin nor that."

THE FIRST SHOT

Madame raises her big rough hands and shrugs her shoulders while Paddy makes a flank attack and gains access to the pantry. He is at last successful, and emerges triumphant with an ample jug.

All this time the bombing class progressed. But we were sadly deficient in materials. Most of our equipment consisted of those amateur Battye bombs, for the manufacture of which a large building had been taken over in Béthune. They were very roughly made of cast iron. We had to cut our own fuses, fix them into the detonators, attach the patent lighter, and wire the whole together, a process involving much labour and delay. The bomb itself, when completed, was highly unsuitable for carriage. But this disadvantage was counterbalanced by the ease with which it could be thrown. It was unfortunate that at this time, and for many months to come, we were not supplied with a standardised grenade. We seemed to be wavering irresolutely between two distinct types, percussion and time-fuse. Those which depended upon percussion for ignition (*e.g.* the Hale) gradually went out of service.

THE FIRST SHOT

They were expensive, cumbersome, and dangerous. The other type, however, increased in favour as its value became more and more impressively manifested. Our first time-fuse grenade, then, was the old Battye, a worthy ancestor to the multiplicity of varieties which appeared from time to time, until, having run through the whole gamut from the light and heavy R.L. to the Pitcher and the Hairbrush, a final selection was made of the Mills. The Mills grenade was at length standardised, and is now in general use, the others having completely disappeared.

Meantime the battalion had for the second time participated in the common dangers of trench life at a place which was known as the Orchard, and on this occasion the task of digging a new line on virgin soil devolving upon it, exposed the battalion to perils not hitherto met. On June 11th it took over again, relieving the appropriate unit of the 154th Brigade, which, as was constantly rumoured, had been selected to force a thrust in the sector of Festubert. The bombing squads by this time had been

THE FIRST SHOT

evolved into a fairly workable unit. But as the trained grenadiers were numerically small, the unit was placed at the disposal of the Brigade for employment on its front, and became known as the Brigade Grenadier Company. In these four officers and in this small company of men was vested a complete monopoly in hand grenades. What is now as necessary to the training of the soldier as the practice of bayonet-fighting or musketry was then thought foolhardy and suicidal in those who ventured to be its expositors. And the apprentice of to-day is as confident in his approach to the science as the apostle of yesterday was apprehensive.

The Brigade Grenadier Company, with whom for the succeeding month I was most intimately concerned, was divided into four squads, each squad representing a battalion and officered by a nominee of that unit.

While the Brigade held the line, the head-quarters of the company were those of Brigade Head-quarters, and every twenty-four hours one squad went on duty in the

THE FIRST SHOT

trenches, the remaining three squads being in billets at the Moat Farm, near the village of Le Touret. Round the outside of the house ran a wide and deep moat, of a green hue and an unwholesome smell. In our own room, bare of furniture except a rickety chair, and lacking all ornament except the inevitable polychrome picture of the Virgin, the ceiling had been perforated by a ragged lump of shrapnel. Shells still dropped with a strange fidelity to programme round our farm, and all we could do was to sit at the window and watch the heavies bursting a short distance away. There is a melancholy attraction about a bursting shell. It is picturesquely horrible. In mid-air a most beautiful cloud of greyish-white smoke suddenly appears, with lamp-black veins. The sudden crash of the explosion strikes fear in the heart, and the spell is broken.

On the night of the 12th Mr. ——–'s party went into the trenches. When it departed, with a general cheerfulness instilled by the smiling presence of its leader, we little knew how soon that gallant leader was to fall. He was mortally wounded on the 13th by a

THE FIRST SHOT

shell, and lived but a few hours. He was carried into the Field Ambulance at Locon, but expired soon after admission, and was buried in the neighbouring cemetery.

FESTUBERT

The poppy-blooded fields are drowsed with sleep,
And just the rustle of a scampering rat
Stirs the rank grasses. Night is fain to weep
Her poisonous dews upon this rotting flat.
A headless body sprawls across my feet,
A trunkless head is gaping through the sod,
A rillet of his blood still smokes with heat . . .
    Is there a God ? Is there a God ?

The gates of Anger open, and the flood,
Spated with hate, unstemmed of men, pours out,
Drenching the trench with hot and beaded blood,
Choking each challenging or anguish'd shout.
And this man's glassy eye is gouged and seared,
And that man's frothing forehead once was broad.
We have our sacrificial pyre upreared . . .
    Is there a God ? Is there a God ?

We are despairing, mad. What matters it ?
Hungry . . . but we can feast in fellowship
On all the horrors of a fever-fit,
And pique them with a palsy-shaken quip.
What is this pulp upon the parados ?
A lettered don, first of his period;
And now his brains are oozing in the fosse . . .
    Is there a God ? Is there a God ?

THE SILENT GUNS

There is a pool thickened with pendant weeds.
A frog sits croaking where a dead man lies,
And his soft hair is circleted with reeds,
And greenish slime is trickling from his eyes.
Lo! once he held a populace in awe,
His Prussian peers took counsel from his nod;
He knew no leash of liberty or law . . .
    Perhaps there *is* a God.

A lark shrills of a sudden, jubilant,
Faint and more faint, and rives the misty shroud;
The dawn is flushing and the westering slant
Of rosy spears is piercing the pent cloud.
And this man's agonising groans no longer call,
And that man's soul has found an easier road,
And the lark's artless singing over all,
    Tells me there *is* a God.

THE rumour prevalent in battalion circles that an attack impended became realised when the 154th Brigade, acting under orders suddenly received, took over the line. Very little was known of the imminent stroke, but as is usual in such cases there was much baseless conjecture. The belief gained a certain amount of currency that the operation was to synchronise with an attack by the French on the German positions between Arras and La Bassée. Not till a whole brigade had been shattered before the enemy's lines did it appear that our attack was a diversion.

Prior to the delivery of the assault the 153rd Brigade went into billets in the vicinity of Locon. The little band of grenadiers with whom I was associated possessed themselves of a farmhouse at La Tombe Willot, tenanted by two young girls, one of whom was a refugee. All that was necessary for our comfort was gladly yielded by these girls, who, besides showing various little acts of kindness, strove to establish a sympathetic liaison by the use of broken English. Forewarned of the approach of a bloody battle, and half suspecting the issue, I now made the strongest endeavours to see my brother, whose battalion, the 4th Seaforths, I had heard was in the vicinity. And after much diligent search and weary travel I found these Ross-shire men at rest in the village of Vieille Chapelle. My brother looked very well and cheerful, even after the nightmare experiences of May 9th. This fortuitous meeting resigned me to the future, which I now awaited with confidence.

The plans for the forthcoming assault

THE SILENT GUNS

developed daily. The bombing personnel of the 154th Brigade, however, was insufficient to cope with the requirements, and in an emergency we were ordered to hold ourselves in instant readiness to support. On the 15th two officers left with fifty men, and I was left alone with the residue, hourly expecting the summons. That night the bombardment swelled to terrible proportions. Looking towards the lines the eye was dazzled with the multitude of lights. Now it was the flash of exploding shells; now it was the slow glare of rockets arching in the sky. Sometimes the crash of the cannon softened into a muttering, when the tattoo of the machine guns became audible. The suspense of waiting was almost unbearable. All through the night the tension was extreme, yet no orders came through to relieve it. The men gathered around in excitable little knots and asked the question a hundred times: What is happening? But the information was too vague, the evidence to support a victory too inconclusive. Victory indeed was in every one's mouth, and if a voice pronounced the hateful word " de-

THE SILENT GUNS

feat " it was suppressed with much indignant protest.

No time for lugubrious observations fell to our lot. On the afternoon of the 16th an urgent message was conveyed to me to report at Brigade Head-quarters with the remainder of the bombing squad. There packs were stacked and our fighting kit reduced to the minimum. The matter seemed to be one of extreme urgency, for a motor-lorry was placed at our disposal. The Brigade-Major gave me final instructions to report at the dump at Le Touret for grenades. We clambered aboard and were driven away to the scene of action. At Le Touret men were feverishly detonating Battye bombs and placing them in roughly fashioned boxes. A thin rain was falling. The candles were guttering. The guns were flashing from the coppices. Not a word was uttered. It seemed as if the spirit of grim, unrelaxing effort had descended upon all. We loaded our wagon with the precious freight of explosives and plunged away over the boggy country roads. I reported to the Brigadier of the 154th Brigade, who was awaiting

ARRAS

the fresh bombers with unabated impatience.

I asked him:

"Where shall I find Scott, sir?"

"I am sorry to say Scott is killed."

"And Harley?"

"Harley, too, I fear has been killed, but messages are as yet obscure, and it may be that he is only wounded."

For a few hours we rested in a farm, a prey to all kinds of misgivings and wondering what evil mischance had befallen our comrades. Then, about midnight, we were supplied with a guide and directed to our posts. We arrived at the trenches at Festubert during the progress of a brigade relief, and I stumbled upon some of my own battalion taking over the line. While day was dawning the mass of soldiers, bending under their accoutrements, slowly unlocked: some to hurry out of the furnace heat of battle, others to face the fiery ordeal. It was impossible to make any progress. I lay down on an ammunition box in an old disused support trench and fell fast asleep. My men were gathered together in a de-

THE SILENT GUNS

serted bay. When order was at length restored I resumed my course. Who could be blind to the horrors, who could be dumb to the cries? The first man I saw was the bombing sergeant, with his head laid open, being carried back on a stretcher, moaning and pleading for water which could not assuage his thirst or moisten his parched throat. The bodies of two Black Watch pipers, their red kilts splashed with blood, lay near. Every little nook was filled by wounded men who had crawled there to die.

I picked my way along the front line to that corner of terror, "L 8." Here a sap, following the line of a natural ditch, twisted out to the German trenches. It was a point of vital importance, and the enemy, with his customary prescience, shelled it till it was ploughed and ploughed again. At this inferno Scott was killed, and another officer desperately wounded in the leg. Their parties had melted before the devastating blast. One squad was blown to pieces when a shell registered a direct hit on a box of hand grenades. Heaps of bodies were mortifying there, so cut up and scattered by the high concentration of shells that it was impossible to distinguish one corpse from another.

On the night of the 17th the attack was resumed on the right with redoubled fury. The 2nd Gordons were ordered to the attack, their first objective being a T-trench jutting out from the German lines. " D " Company of the Gordons, linking up with the sister battalion, went over the parapet and advanced to the enemy's position to make a feint demonstration and distract his attention from the real assault. But it was labour in vain. The 2nd Gordons hammered ineffectual blows, and, melting before the sleet of lead, collapsed at the wire. A gallant remnant, however, succeeded in gaining a precarious footing in the T-trench. Meanwhile, " D " Company, miraculously preserved from heavy casualties, had returned to the original line. They found No Man's Land full of decaying corpses; but not all corpses. They succoured wounded men who had lain out for days, suffering all the agonies of thirst and enduring the stench of their own mortifying injuries. Here Captain (then

Lieutenant) Robert Ross, Banchory, one of the finest men I have had the honour to know, performed an act of conspicuous courage, returning in the face of a murderous fire to carry in a man who had been terribly wounded some days previously, and had been given up for dead. This poor fellow was well-nigh insensible, and so dazed and broken that he begged to be left to die where he fell. Beside him, drenched in blood, sprawled a dead German, probably his victim. Ross was recommended for decoration, and received the Military Cross.

Towards morning the struggle quietened down. Our guns were silent. *They had no more shells to fire.* Even the prodigal Germans were breathing freely. A lark rose from the ground and sang . . . and sang . . , and sang, as if its little throat would burst. The frogs were croaking in a ditch. Impelled by curiosity I stole over to watch them. There were two men in the ditch, rotting. I crept back, shuddering with disgust. It was time to stand to. One man was asleep, his head resting on his chest. " Come, my man," I said to him kindly,

THE SILENT GUNS

for I knew he had received no food, and sleep was a blessed release to the torture, "come now, stand to," and passed on. My fine men were all alert. Returning, I found my friend still in the posture of slumber, and, seizing his shoulder, I shook him roughly, for duty must sink all sympathy in a crisis. But his head fell still lower, and, as he pitched forward at my feet, limp and motionless, I turned up his face . . . and it was the face of a dead man. I went on my rounds. Like Macbeth, I had "supped full with horrors."

At 3 a.m. a company of guardsmen, laden with Hale grenades, suddenly appeared in the trench. One of their officers, noticing me standing near, approached and said:

"Hullo! When are you going over?"

"Going over? I don't understand."

"What! Do you mean to say you don't know you're attacking this morning?"

"Well, it's the first time I've heard it."

Looking over the parapet:

"You're attacking all right, and we're helping you." Then, meditatively: "Five hundred yards . . . ditches you can't jump . . . and the poor devils have to carry scaling

THE SILENT GUNS

ladders . . . wire uncut . . . and " (pointing back to the guns with savage heat) " not a *damned* shell. . . . My God ! " That is how battles were fought in those days.

The guardsmen disappeared out of the trench as silently and quickly as they had entered it. It seemed that their information was not at fault. We were to have attacked, but the hour was postponed till five o'clock. Arrangements were hurriedly made to cope with the new situation. Bridging parties were detailed to span the ditches in No Man's Land. We waited for food. None appeared. We took the bully-beef out of dead men's haversacks and ate it ravenously. The minutes crept by slowly. Some of us resigned ourselves to the inevitable, and slept for a short time. Our one hope lay in the guns. Four o'clock, and the guns were still silent. Half-past four, and not a single shell whined to our assistance. A quarter to five, ten minutes to five, and the German gunners, prescient as usual, opened on our crowded trenches. In imagination we saw the enemy squinting along the sights of his machine guns ready to sweep down in broad

THE SILENT GUNS

daylight all living things that dared to cross that intervening strip of hell.

But the attack, which would have been a madman's act, did not materialise. At the last moment it was cancelled. The tension over, all of us who could lay down and fell fast asleep. "Sleep," says Leigh Hunt, " is perhaps Nature's never-failing relief, as swooning is upon the rack. Without meaning to lessen the dignity of suffering which has quite enough to do with its waking hours, it is this that may often account for the profound sleeps enjoyed the night before hazardous battles, executions, and other demands upon an over-excited spirit." We ate what little breakfast we could scrape together with enviable relish. Even the ghastly sights and sounds had now no terrors, and the men were preparing their meals beside the heaps of unburied bodies as if nothing in the world had happened. The enemy gunfire rolled persistently, and claimed victims every hour. A high proportion of casualties was inflicted on the officers. In the course of the morning Lieutenant Innes, a veteran of South Africa, was killed, and three officers wounded.

THE SILENT GUNS

Having restored its mental and physical stability by a short rest at Cornet Malo, the battalion again came to grips in trenches contiguous to those which had been marked by such a bloody slaughter during the previous week. These trenches may collectively be called India Village, as they had winter associations with our dusky auxiliaries. The Brigade Grenadier Company, reconstituted, returned on June 22nd to the Moat Farm, its officer personnel having been complemented. In its new form, however, it was shortlived. It was recognised that such a small body at the service of the whole brigade was too impracticable. These grenadier specialists, therefore, were disbanded to their various units. But the formation had not been in vain. The idea was to germinate and bear fruit.

At this time my trench journal reads:

"*June* 23rd.—Not much of a rest here. The Brigade Grenadier Company ceases to exist from to-day. We are sorry after a fashion, because to-night we leave our homely tenement and rejoin our battalions. It feels like parting from accustomed haunts, an

THE SILENT GUNS

exile's feelings: 'Nos dulcia linquimus arva, nos patriam fugimus.' Dusk. The unlovely lights of war stabbing the sky. The sigh of a shell on the wind. We troop down to the trenches in single file, across an open flat, and through the ruins of a village (India Village), and now a sand-bag shelter and a little head-cover, and I can sleep as it was in the venturous days of old, when—

> '. . . Weariness can snore
> Upon the stony flint when resty sloth
> Finds the down pillow hard . . .'"

"*June 24th.*—The outlook from our position is very circumscribed. 'A' Company is in support. To attain it we pass through a communication trench half a mile long, broken up here and there by shells, and frequently intersected by ditches of rotting water. An old German trench crosses it at right angles. Some of the dug-outs of this trench were palaces, but now it is one long cemetery. No uncommon sight to see a withered hand or part of a head sticking out of the clay after the rains have washed down the deposits. . . . Busy myself in excavating a niche in the clay, large enough to sit in with comfort, and having a little gallery for a candle. Shielding the light with a waterproof sheet I can read at night if such is my inclination. All night long the men sally out and in, repairing their trenches and making good fire positions. For a time I sit in my niche and read the *Luck of the Vails*. That and my bijou New Testament are my only literature. To-morrow I shall throw the ' Luck ' over the parapet."

The bitter dolour of the shambles at Festubert, though not present in the visible form of death, was here intensified by the hearse-like quiet. The skies were already overcast when we took over, and hardly had our shovels commenced to strengthen the position when a dreadful and prolonged rainfall set in, flooding the trenches and heaping discomfort on discomfort. In those early days nobody knew the meaning of the word " dug-out." We counted it lucky to be able to scrape a niche in the mud and creep in there to hide the utter weariness of our bodies. No. 4 Communication Trench, full of offensive smells, and, on account of its

THE SILENT GUNS

extreme length, both irksome and dangerous, became nothing more than a mere waterlogged ditch.

A change-over occurred on the 25th. Our new lines straddled the Quinque Rue at Festubert, the right flank resting on No. 2 Communication Trench. But two days later, on a brilliant Sunday, the 4th Battalion (Inverness Territorial) of the Cameron Highlanders relieved us, and we marched out to billet and bivouac near La Gorgue. It was a villainously slow march. The bitter cold chilled us, and when at last we threw down our packs we had no shelter except the ceiling of the stars. Two officers slept in a disused fly, to the extreme amusement of Madame the next morning, who shrugged her shoulders and laughed, saying: " Oh, la! la! " Then the laugh softened a little and the corners of the lips drooped. " Ces pauvres, ils vient d'arriver des trrranchées. Ils sont fatigués. Ils ont faim." Already the company batmen were astir. " Hey, Madame, Oofs." And soon the omelette was heard spluttering—that eternal omelette, but how sweet and palatable!

THE SILENT GUNS

The folly of hearkening to idle report was never more triumphantly proved than now. It had been in the mouth of everybody that another week would see us at Armentières, or even farther north still. The rumour did not go bare and ungarnished. The most unlikely things were prophesied, and, what is more remarkable, implicitly believed. The most outrageous lies were circulated to the detriment of the truth. Before the week was old the exact date of our leaving the western front and embarking for INDIA had been determined to the complete satisfaction of every mess, and no one dared to dispute a rumour which had emanated from the padre and had received his benediction.

The Division did *not* go to Armentières. Nor did it proceed farther north. It took over trenches in the sector of Laventie. And it was to the town of Laventie that the battalion now went to billet. Laventie had been entered by the Germans in October 1914, and vacated after the lapse of six days owing to the pressure of stronger forces or in conformity with the general plan. Although separated from the front line at a distance of only three miles, it was still inhabited by many of the citizens, principally on the outskirts of the town. The centre of this place, from which radiated all the chief roads, was marked by the ruins of the church, a mere shell, and as sad a spectacle as could be witnessed in all this martyred region. True to their faith, many of the Catholics still clung to their dearest possessions, and one cannot fail to remember the brave nuns of the Hospice, who refused to abandon their infirm charges to the fury of the oppressor.

The trenches in the sector of Laventi partook of the nature of breastworks, and were in a much better state of repair than those of Festubert and Richebourg L'Avoué. It would seem that the fighting in this quarter had not attained the same infuriate heat as elsewhere. The temporary fever during the operations for the seizure of Aubers Ridge had subsided, but the enemy still held the commanding ground; and our line, forming a wide but not a deep re-entrant, skirted the base of the ridge from Fauquissart to Neuve Chapelle. The sub-sector of Chapigny became our immediate care. The defensive system, on the whole, seemed to be too insecure and vulnerable. Its liability to rupture, if subjected to the intensity of a bombardment and the crushing weight of a massed attack, appeared obvious to everybody. There was but one main line of trenches running parallel to the Rue Tilleloy, but in rear a succession of isolated forts, adequately served, fenced off this fertile country from the onsets of the enemy. Four of these fortified redoubts were strung along the Tilleloy Road from Chapigny to Fauquissart, and a fifth was isolated slightly to the rear.

It was a task, therefore, of the first importance to provide an adequate defensive trench system, and the Highland Division began to prove itself active in the necessary labour. The Germans, on the other hand, from whom we were separated at an average interval of 150 yards, possessed all the natural favours of the ridge. They had at least a *triple* belt of defence, with the additional advantage of numerous communication trenches. Behind their front line were farms capable of being put into a very solid

THE SILENT GUNS

state of defence, such as Ferme Deleval, Trivelet, La Distillerie, Les Mottes Ferme, and the Moulin du Pietre. As their line receded, the trees grew more and more abundantly, wherein they were able to conceal large numbers of guns. They had also the inestimable advantage of full observation from the ridge. Surmounting this high ground lay the village of Aubers, fed by a light railway. This natural bulwark, in the hands of skilful troops, could resist the strongest frontal pressure that could be brought to bear upon it.

On July 16th the 5th Seaforths relieved my battalion, the enemy doing his utmost to interfere. Having the range of the roads that approached our trenches, he loosed off thousands of rounds, fitfully spraying the pathways in the hope of catching us unawares. In this he was unsuccessful, but many times we were forced to lie low till the firing moderated. The night was fine, and it was a strange line of ghostly figures that crossed the open fields, making for the high road to Laventie, dimly seen in the distance as a few fickle rays of moonlight filtered through the clouds and lit upon it. A march of an hour and a half brought us to La Gorgue-Estaires, where, we were informed, billets awaited us. By 1 a.m. the whole battalion was accommodated in a deserted factory on the banks of the River Lys, here very filthy and undesirable. Tired men take very little time to make themselves at home, and we were not worried by the usual disturbance of taking over strange billets in the dark. House-room for the officers was much more difficult of accomplishment. And in my own case, the proprietor to whom I had been allotted by the billeting officer had retired early for the night. Result: at 2 a.m. an acrimonious squabble between myself and my unwilling host, who leant half way out of an upstairs window and waved his bare arms. The question was settled, weakly on our part because we were too wearied to enforce our rights, by an adjournment to the estaminet of the Ear of Corn, " A L'Epi de Blé," where the wildest rumours were current about the capitulation of Turkey and the fall of La Bassée. The landlord was very obliging, and put two

THE CHURCH OF ESTAIRES AND THE
RIVER LYS

THE SILENT GUNS

rooms at our disposal, where we slept very soundly till well into the next day. This billet being provisional, we transferred our valises to the " Belle Vue " Estaminet.

From the 21st the Division fully implemented its promise of giving the battalion a good rest. In a beautiful grassy orchard of Caudescure, a hamlet not many kilometres from Merville, we remained perfectly free from the curse of endless parades and fatigue parties and alarms. But these halcyon days could not last. At 9.45 a.m. on the 26th we marched *via* St. Venant to Berguettes, twelve miles distant on the Nord Railway, and there entrained. The good offices of Salaun were requisitioned to ensure a supply of the best local vintage, and resulted in a *succès fou*. During the whole of that tiresome journey we never ceased to pledge our eternal gratitude for this benevolent act. We passed westward through Hazebrouck and St. Omer, west into the night, which crept slowly over the flats, deeper and darker, until the twinkling lights of Calais and the fresh fair faces of women steeped us in reveries of home.

V   EXTENDING THE LINE

THE first greys of morning were just showing through the trees like striated patchwork when the sleepy-eyed battalion, once freed from the choking confinement of the wagons, stretched its stiffening limbs and breathed a purer air. First impressions are as a rule deceptive, but our first impressions of the Somme, when we detrained that morning at Méricourt-Ribemont, lingered for many a day as a sweet memory. The period that followed was one of inestimable preciousness to us. The free wholesomeness of the air, the fresh breezes that served but to stir the leaves and ruffle the pools, contrasted strangely with the clogging miasmas of Flanders. We felt ourselves excited with the discovery of a new world. The whole landscape in our appreciative eyes appeared to be lapped with a beauty as yet untarnished by the impurities of war. The burnishing skies

EXTENDING THE LINE

were tricked out with a new colouring. In the north the dawn came up with splendours that were hidden from us. The mists blinded the sunrise in Flanders.

An officer who had motored south to arrange the billets met us at the station with rosy accounts of our new area. His reception had been violently enthusiastic, because the good people of Picardy, observing the kilt for the first time, lionised the wearer till (as he said) he blushed for shame. The natives were all agog with excitement to acclaim the "ladies from hell." He had undergone a testing catechism of questions on the subject of his Highland uniform, a topic of unending interest to the French, and we were to expect a most exhaustive scrutiny from which we could not, as befitted a traditionally bold regiment, retreat without grave loss of prestige. So the prophets! We marched away from the leafy arches of Méricourt, that seemed to entreat the tired traveller to revel in their coolnesses. New vistas opened out before us. On our right hand a sugar refinery shot its well-known ugly chimney into the skies. On our left hand a roadside shrine, all muffled in greenery, seemed to implore a moment's meditation. But there, in front, joy to our hearts, lay the broad rolling uplands, topped with yellowing corn that went before the breeze in glistening waves. There were a few early harvesters at work—old men with sunken cheeks and women with toiling hands, who came half shyly to look at the strange creatures in petticoats and listen to the weird music of the pipes. *Picardy will never forget the kilt. The pipes will never cease to sound.*

A new wonder now brought amazement to our faces—those marvellous national highways, that take no account of contours, but run ruler-straight for miles. That on which we set foot at this time was known as the " Route Nationale No. 29 de Rouen." From Albert to Amiens it ran with scarcely a single deflection. And, as was a feature common to all these national roads, magnificent trees bordered it from end to end. Even in the cases of secondary roads attempts were made to utilise the waste lands contiguous. Apple and plum trees were growing by the roadside, their boughs bending with fast ripening fruit. They were all communally owned. We Scots are twitted and teased about our exceeding thriftiness, but, indeed, we do not know the meaning of the word. The properest school of thriftiness is France.

The battalion went into billets in the quaint little village of Franvillers. It was not an elegant village. Its houses all looked jerry-built; its streets affected no definite direction, but seemed to have been irregularly conceived. Franvillers was the communal centre of a large agricultural district. There were no isolated, outlying farms. All were collected within the boundaries of the village, in order to ensure mutual protection. Each house in the village had its barns and its byres attached. One man was no richer than his neighbour, and there was no incitement to ambition. The men who remained, not subject to the military levies, were all old men. About the village the most distinguished person was the *curé*. I spoke with him once, having occasion to pay a call, as our Breton interpreter, M. Salaun, was billeted in his house. Unexpected contact with him gave one the idea of a mysteriously grand aloofness and stern piety to which by means of sacerdotal exclusion and a strict regimen of conduct he had gradually attained. But when one came face to face with his housekeeper, a fat, puffy woman and visibly addicted to snuff, all fine impressions vanished.

Captain —— stayed with me in the best billet that I had till this moment the pleasure of occupying. The house, a small one, covered the heads of four people. M. Bertoux, cultivateur, being too old to figure in the active army, had been sent down to Amiens in connection with some military duties. The oldest son, Réné, who had been twice kissed by Papa Joffre for gallant behaviour in the field, was fighting at Les Eparges, near Verdun. Madame Bertoux, a very kind and sympathetic woman, like all other French wives took the war calmly. Grandpère and Léopold added two more to this interesting family. But since my arrival in France I had seen no one who could approach in the matter of simple gentility and innocence, Germaine, the daughter of Madame Bertoux. Germaine had eighteen years. She told me so herself. She was a brunette of a type unusually rare, with a small round face and dancing eyes. Her teeth were perfect. There was an incomparable frugality about this family. They were their own dressmakers and their own provision merchants. Germaine contrived some wonderful dresses out of whatever materials could be bought by infrequent visits to Amiens.

On the 31st all the officers were assembled together and addressed by the Colonel. We were going to relieve a battalion of the 44th French Brigade of Infantry, recruited from Brittany and possessed of martial traditions no less renowned than our own. All that could help to promote the *entente cordiale* was to be encouraged. As long as we were in touch with them, the bonds of sympathy were to be cemented by every possible means. It was at length decided to send two officers per company into the line for instruction, so that, having familiarised themselves with its peculiarities, they would be able to guide in the battalion and put it on its guard against danger points.

From Franvillers to Bécourt was a distance tediously long, and a start at 3 p.m. was not deemed too early in order to reach our objective before dark. But the day was oppressively hot, and our packs were very heavy indeed. The roads, so undeviating, although they traversed the most beautiful agricultural scenery, by reason of that very directness did not make our task less severe. To our delight a long French wagon clattered up empty. The whole party, twelve in number, dashed up to seize the opportunity, shouting atrocious French to a driver, whose staring eyes saw nothing but swinging kilts, and whose ears could not have interpreted a single syllable of our speech. Finally a seductive glance achieved the impossible. The shapeless wagon rumbled to a jarring stop, and we all clambered aboard, full of gratitude to this nameless rustic. Our loaded *camion* rolled merrily over hill and down dale, to the intense astonishment of the Frenchwomen harvesting. Peals of honest laughter sounded at the graceless display of hunched-up knees. Up and down, up and down, every jolt of the cumbrous, springless cart shaking the bones almost out of our bodies. In the end we arrived at an estaminet one kilometre from our place of report, and, the time being much more than ample, we sat down in what was called the Officers' Mess of Dernancourt, to drink coffee till it was time to proceed farther.

We reported to Brigade Head-quarters at Moulin du Vivier, a mill lapped round by the most profound quiet, under whose shallow culverts slowly flowed the Ancre. Here final instructions were issued, and English-speaking guides came to assist us in the work of relief. It was remarkable how many of these poilus spoke English. Indeed, the majority of those who professed acquaintance with our language spoke it with fluency and a nice distinction of idiom. Méaulte was full of the blue képis. All the fine impressionable fellows of France came out to welcome us. On passing out of the village, our guides, alert to dangers, paused ere we took the high road, and finally appealed to us that we must keep to the natural defile, which at this point led on to Bécordel.

At Bécordel, just under the arch which carries the light railway to Guillemont and Combles, the first trench began. Here, however, it was an expedient to avoid needless casualties from dropping shots rather than a necessity for defence. Enfilade machine-gun fire from La Boisselle, down what latterly came to be known as Sausage Valley, was often a fruitful source of wearing down our rifle strength by the indirect process of attrition. And this trench, into which we now set foot, was designed, if not to obviate the danger, at least to reduce it to the minimum. Past a wayside Calvary, where the body of a French major reposed, his days of fighting over for ever, and up a winding carriage drive, we entered the courtyard of Bécourt Château, at one time the home of the Count of Valicourt, who, many years before, had held the portfolio of the Ministry of Arboriculture. In the yard we encountered an excited group of Frenchmen, all very anxious to show their native hospitality to the allies, all speaking at once, all gesticulating. Among them the commandant was effusively courteous.

"Velcome, messieurs," said the commandant. "You are come from ze nort', n'est-ce pas? From Festubert! Ah! Ce sont de mauvaises tranchées, comme celles du Labyrinthe, trrrrès acharnées. How you say? Ha! Bloody! Oui, oui, assurément, zat ees ze . . . ze mot."

The major, speaking in all seriousness, uttered the words so expressively that his coppery moustaches bristled, and a sous-lieutenant, acquainted with the idiom of the English language, saw the *double entendre* and burst into laughter.

"My Commandant," he said, "it is not of the politest, that word. But, ma foi, it is true."

"Zut! C'est bien vrai, mon enfant. Mais par ici, ze tranchées, zey are tranquilles. Ze Boches, zey have not made von leetle at-tack. Ve have ze gourbis, oh, magnifiques! and ze vines, vous en allez goûter."

When he had finished speaking, as if to give the lie to his words, a loud explosion reverberated down the valley, and a fine haze of smoke, like that from a fire on a calm day, spread out over the distant tree-tops.

" Ours ? " asked one of our captains.

" Mon Dieu, non. Ce sont des torpilles aériennes à La Boisselle."

" So," interrupted the French artillery liaison officer, " attendez ! "

We waited. About forty seconds passed. Then the angry bark of the seventy-fives, the scream of the shells, and the faultless bursts broke upon the silence and left us mute and wondering. Who could not help thinking of Festubert ?

The consultation at Head-quarters between the French officers and their guests was largely shared by the poilus, who surrounded their superiors and interrupted their sentences either with enthusiastic bravos or vehement deprecations. If the Major decided that " A " Company should relieve by way of the Boyau Lenharée, it would not have been extraordinary to hear Corporal Jacques arguing with him that the Boyau Besançon was a safer and more accessible way. Dusk was creeping over Bécourt Wood. The

THE SMOKE OF BATTLE

EXTENDING THE LINE

flowers, growing with sad profusion on the numerous graves in the garden, were closing. In the line, sentry groups were being posted, and everybody assuming a wary and suspicious expression. Major Dawson, impatiently listening to a seemingly endless conversation, was plucking my arm and begging me to find the guide who should take us to our trench quarters. We found him. He spoke English fairly well, having been in the onion trade and travelled frequently to Wales. He was very communicative, and vastly proud to have been chosen for this duty.

The work of taking over was always a strange proceeding. All we saw was the flash of a fusee; all we heard was the whine of a bullet. These were trenches such as we had never experienced hitherto. In the north we had been accustomed to sandbagged breastworks; but here the trenches were deep, and wound serpent-wise in a fashion that left the stranger utterly bewildered. It was a labyrinthine system, constructed according to the suggestion of the natural contours, and not following a stereotyped plan as at the Quinque Rue. On first acquaintance with these amazing passages it was impossible to move about with any assurance whatever. Not until a lengthy residence therein had made us familiar with the mazes could we walk about with a perfect sense of direction. The communication trenches crossed each other, doubled back, affected the most bizarre forms.

My diary illustrates the nature of these places. It reads :

"*July* 30*th*.—It is in such places that whole armies have lived all winter, relieved only at irregular periods. In the parados men have dug holes, where, two by two, they sleep like dogs in kennels, a curtain of rough sacking fixed by a rusty bayonet serving as a protection from wind and rain and sun. Inside, one eats, sleeps, sings. And sometimes dies. The shelters of the officers are a little larger, and the first-aid posts have the choice of security. Each company has its telephone and telegraph instruments. A liaison is established between all posts of command. . . . Here men are reading, others are writing home those

EXTENDING THE LINE

few words of solace that mothers and sweethearts alone kiss for their preciousness. There a stretcher bearer is binding up a wound. By raising the head a corner of blue sky can be seen. Yes, the sky can be blue, too, at the front, and the flowers can bloom and the birds can sing."

By 9.30 —— and myself were in the firing line, royally entertained. The officers messed surprisingly well, and we found that they were able to get a great many things from Albert. Dinner in the firing line was an event undreamed of, but here the cuisine was not only excellent but abundant, and the Medoc imposed a warm geniality, and we opened our hearts one to the other and joked as if there were no enemy within miles.

A trifle fatigued I accompanied the aspirant of the 10th Company to rest. In the French Army the aspirant is one who " aspires " to commissioned rank and completes his apprenticeship in the field. He is a cadet who learns in the school of reality. The aspirant who now took me to his dug-out and showed me the rough couch of wire netting where I should lie down to sleep,

EXTENDING THE LINE

was M. Allégret, a licentiate in law of Paris University and one time French Vice-Consul in Japan. Before turning in himself, he questioned the patrol sergeant with a minuteness that astonished me. The following morning I awoke early, with the intention of making myself familiar with the sector we were to occupy. Viewed in the clear light of day the new trenches presented every moment fresher aspects, and the delighted mind could never tire of the work of exploration. Now it was a piece of chalk carving, in which the French Tommies were vastly skilled; now it was a welcoming banneret, such as " Piton shakes hands with the British Tommy."

Everything was as quiet and silent as the grave. We could look over the parapet and gaze down Sausage Valley and see the gaping wreck of La Boisselle, a few blasted trees and fallen bricks. The Frenchmen never spoke of La Boisselle without tears in their eyes. Inch by inch they had won forward, but, exhausted with the effort, could not drive the stubborn enemy out of the terrible warren of the village. And now,

EXTENDING THE LINE

when they were leaving, they charged us to hold those sacred sepulchres and defend them with our dead bodies. The pact was kept. But at what a cost!

From a certain angle the damaged campanile of the church of Albert just showed over Bécourt Wood. It used to present a marvellously fine sight, that gilded statue so perilously depending, and, when the morning rays of the sun lighted upon it, it shone like a very jewel in the sky. We have read tales of the firing line, both poignant and merry. Humour has flashed through the gloom; horrors have been served up with a pique of fun; but there are things in France to-day that defy all attempts at a jest, where a smile would be an impertinence and laughter a sacrilege. They are the ruins. While the sorrows of men can be assuaged, the sorrows of dumb nature are eternal. The ruins will remain ruins till the end of all time. Even when the crumbling walls are builded, and once more resound with the careless hum of life, the ghosts of the fallen stones will remain. Soldiers for the first time going up to the line, and seasoned

EXTENDING THE LINE

veterans returning to rest, regard the ruins from very different standpoints. On each class the wreckage makes a different appeal. The first ruins I ever saw in France were those of the Rue de Bois near Festubert. My companion, now asleep in the soldiers' cemetery of Le Touret, turned to me and said in his broad Aberdeenshire doric: "Fa'd ha' thocht it? Man, we'll hae to pey the deevils back for't." In his mind revenge was uppermost.

But those coming out of the line are oppressed with a sense of awful tragedy. The mind relieved from the personal feeling of danger is brought to regard the paralysing horror of the fallen stones. The very breath shudders. The reflected light of far-distant Very flares throws an intangible veil of witchery round them. Who of all the countless brave whose feet have wakened vain empty echoes in the desolated decaying streets of Neuville St. Vaast, whose eyes have not shrunk from the ghastliness of the Labyrinth, whose ears could hear the mine so fearfully near, has not felt arrowy pangs shoot through his heart when his gaze fell

EXTENDING THE LINE

upon Mont St. Eloi? It stands out against the sky. The rough serration of its edge seems to cut into the clouds. The whole front teems with such ruins. The matchless cathedral of Rheims, not less than the mediaeval Cloth Hall of Ypres, draws tears to the eyes.

The same feeling assailed one in Albert. On a moonlight night, when the broken city lay in the palest and filmiest of veils, looking down upon it from the hill of Bécourt and beyond towards the white chalky trenches streaking La Boisselle and Ovillers, the falling Madonna of the church, with gilded arms piteously outswept, used to chill the heart. This is surely one of the most pathetic of all ruins.

In August of 1915, just at the time when we relieved the Bretons, it used to be my custom of an evening to drink wine at a little estaminet in the Rue d'Amiens. The *patronne* was inelegant, but her phrases were expressively turned, and she could throw into a single word, to the accompaniment of magical gestures, that depth of meaning of which her beautiful tongue is capable. She was standing one evening as usual, serving the last Breton. I slipped in quietly. One of the marmites had just burst in the square, scattering bricks and paving stones. She said not a word, but, grasping both our arms, went to the door and pointed up to the statue of the Virgin and Child hanging from the basilica. Then she poured out a little wine for each of us, and for herself she took a thimbleful . . . "Trinquez," she said; "à la revanche!" And with that she set about preparing an omelette for Piton.

Some of the ruins are majestic in their very dust. There is more sanctity in the rubble of the cathedral of Arras than ever there was at its inviolate altars. The ugly squat church of Hebuterne no longer exists, but its ground is holier. All the masses that ever were said at Notre Dame de Lorette have not sanctified it more than the splendid blood spilt there like water. Other ruins are reminiscent of sweet things—home life, courtships, children. What can heal such sorrows? Not the vaunted German Kultur, not the panacea of Geibel:

> " Und es mag am deutschen Wesen
> Einmal noch die Welt genesen."

EXTENDING THE LINE

My examination of the trenches, which until now had been of a perfunctory character, now became more pressing. The battalion had been guided into its new quarters on the first day of August, to the intense admiration of the poilus, who were all dying of curiosity to examine our kilts, a curiosity which did not go entirely ungratified. Those who professed to know English interpreted for their less favoured comrades. The others, who were unable to speak our tongue, put an eloquent, if dumb, interrogatory into that peculiarly French aptitude for verbal movement. Temporarily transferred to "D" Company, which was in reserve, I had better opportunities of committing to memory the meshes of this gigantic net. A definite system had been followed in naming the trenches. But the system differed from that which evolved Plug Street out of Ploegsteert. In these French lines a far more romantic plan was adopted. Officers or men who had given their lives in some conspicuous fashion for France, often had their valour perpetuated in the name of a trench. For instance, two brothers of the name of

EXTENDING THE LINE

Honorat fell here in action. Their father, a Breton burning with revenge, volunteered for action, was accepted, and sent to the same regiment. He, too, was killed. Such conspicuous devotion to duty was recalled by the name of one of those trenches, the Tranchée Honorat. A major, whose body lay behind the lines under what the religious call a "Christ" or a "Calvary," in like manner gave his name to one of the principal communication trenches, the Boyau Besançon. We dullards did not think of such a beautiful way of recording valour. We even committed a vandal's act in altering all those names. Perhaps, however, we were more profoundly and lastingly conscious of what we owed to our dead :

> "They passed, they passed, but cannot pass away,
> And England feels them in her blood like wine."

Were we the gainers by the drastic change made in them? From a practical military point of view the results were good. Here was a Territorial battalion actually reproducing on the blood-soaked field of

EXTENDING THE LINE

battle the names familiar to its childhood, elated to feel that it was so chosen to hand down to posterity a record of its achievements thus enshrined.

For twenty-one days we held "E" sector, and during that time, so peaceful was the outlook, we might have been cloistered in a monastery. The hours of daylight passed idly by, and the muteness of the night was almost that of the tomb. It was not even considered worth while to change the position of the companies after the appropriate interval. "A" Company on the right were approached to be relieved by "D," but, not desiring the incidental trouble of interruption, they protested, with some judgment, that any alteration of the existing dispositions could not prove more salutary. They therefore begged to be left alone in the firing line. Their appeal was respected, and "D" Company remained in reserve.

For two days I lived in a dug-out excavated out of the hard white chalk in the Tranchée Honorat. To me it appeared a palace, and indeed, coming as we did from the abominable shelters of evil-smelling sand-bags to which we had been accustomed in Flanders, I accepted the tenancy of this dug-out with delight. But two others arriving as reinforcements, and being posted to our company, a readjustment had to be made, and some of us sought quarters elsewhere. These were decided upon under a large tree growing by the then disused road from Bécourt to La Boisselle. Here Bon Accord Street, following the outline of Bécourt Wood, suddenly terminated. It was truly a wretched shelter, being completely pervious to the rains, exposed to every draught that blew, and hardly proof against the bullets which, fortunately for our lives, always drummed into the tree overhead. At this stage, perhaps, my diary will be found to record most sympathetically the story of these trenches. As Rousseau prefaces this remark in his *Confessions* : " I am sensible the reader has no occasion to know all this, but I feel a kind of necessity for relating it." The entries proceed to relate how on

"*August 2nd.*—I applied myself in my lost moments to the industrious study of carpentry. We required a table and two chairs in order that our meals might be served in comfort. Our chiefest difficulty was lack of materials and tools, the two essentials of the most primeval art. The problem arose how to make a table without planks, without nails, without a hammer. Ogilvie retrieved from the rubbish-heap, as he said, an old French ration box. We had our suspicions that this box had been designed for more ambitious uses than Maconochie, or whatever the French equivalent may be (*singe* is it not?), and we said nothing. Ogilvie extracted sufficient nails to erect a serviceable table, and, having 'borrowed' some chevaux-de-frise from the R.E. stores and denuded it of wire, rested the boards on top of it, and *voilà!* our table. I am to be up all night, but I have a sufficiency of literature to while away the tedium. If the Boches permit me to read my dug-out should not be the most uncomfortable place in the world.

"*August 3rd.*—My dug-out was very cold

last night. One cannot expect much warmth seven feet or more underground, in a bed made of taut wire netting, usually full of holes and swung like a hammock. Even with the additional luxury of a pillow, composed of a sand-bag stuffed with grass, one cannot afford to be a braggart, for up in the firing line the captain has actually got a real bed in his dug-out, and when he awakes in the morning he has a mirror to shave by, and curtains to remind him of home, and windows to let the first rays of the sun stream in, and an arm-chair to rest in when he feels inclined, and a flower vase adorned with all the beautiful wild flowers that luxuriate on the parados. After all, perhaps my cold, draughty wire bed is the more sanitary. I told —— that it was not to my taste to sleep in a mildewy bed, but he only chuckled, and said that verily the grapes were sour.

"*August 6th.*—Heavy rain in the forenoon, which made extensive movement in the trenches impossible, and tended to keep both sides fairly quiet.

"*August 7th.*—The usual outbursts of the mitrailleuse—the 'sewing-machine,' as the

French call it, after the tric-trac of its action. It sprays our parapet nightly. . . . 11 p.m. Two mines of a large size have just been exploded somewhere on our left, probably at La Boisselle. They shook our puny dug-out to its foundations. A very violent artillery bombardment has commenced. In the debatable region of the mines a thick curtain of shrapnel is falling.

"*August 9th.*—1 a.m. The artillery has now died down, but the Germans are restless, and bestir themselves to annoy us by musketry fusillades.

"*August 12th.*—No incident of any importance characterised the 11th, a genial serenity of weather helping to dry up the more exposed parts of the trench, but still leaving wet those that are overshadowed by the woods. All this forenoon, however, we were engaged in draining operations in a communication trench which was called, with a singular appropriateness, the Boyau Rossi. For a long time everything looked so unutterably calm that I was tempted out of the trench into the wood and relaxed my mind with reading. After lunch, bent on securing literature which might have escaped the rapacity of previous occupants, I hurried to the château and disappeared upstairs. Destruction here had followed quickly on the heels of destruction, and the winds were sucked in through huge gaping holes in the walls, and everything bore the marks of wanton ill-usage. I found a deal more books than I expected to find, principally of a devotional character and of little use to any one of my religious persuasion, but a brother officer, who is a Roman Catholic, picked up several missals and prayer-books beautifully bound and printed.

" In the afternoon it rained heavily. Our ramshackle dug-out became unstable, and allowed the rain to percolate through the roof and flood us out of bed and board, a scurvy trick which we made haste to remedy. There was a small dug-out hard by, recently constructed by the engineers, but unfurnished. This we appropriated, and by forced labour succeeded in introducing two wire beds into its narrow confines. In the intervals of fine weather we carried out the flitting, so that quite early in the night we had comfortable accommodation in our new *Mulviross Villa*. I am coveting some heavy hangings from the château to adorn the villa, and with only reasonable luck we shall yet outrival the Captain.

"*August* 18*th*.—3 a.m. During the last two hours a heavy mist has settled in the valley (*i.e.* Sausage Valley). This is a real test of nerves, and the Germans are obviously suffering. A heavy rifle fire is sustained in case we are attempting to profit by the prevailing conditions.

"*August* 19*th*.—A thick white mist has again clothed the valley in an impenetrable bank, to the great discomfiture of the Germans. Heavy volume of rifle-fire till dawn, when the mist rising and disclosing no hostile movement each side regains its composure and settles down to sleep. . . . 11 p.m. Three hours ago a large mine was exploded which, judging by the reverberation and the earth tremor, must have produced considerable damage on whatever front the explosion occurred. The ensuing uneasiness to which the enemy was keyed infected the artillery, and a heavy duel fol-

lowed which lasted well into the night. . . .
Midnight.—Term of duty over. I rouse up
——. He is loath to rise and very sleepy,
but we boil some water and make some toddy,
and eat white puddings till I am inclined
to sleep and he is prepared for his vigil."

On the 24th we were relieved by the 5th
Seaforths, with whom we were soon to have
very intimate relations in the routine matter
of relieving, when confidence in the efficiency
of both parties meant a heartier co-operation.
If, for example, one battalion regarded its
successor in the line with disfavour, if there
existed any petty rivalry (for this was not
unknown), or if reliance could not be placed
on the undertaking of the incoming unit to
continue the work in progress, then there
was not the same incentive to honest labour.
But the greatest cordiality marked our relations with the 5th Seaforths. Trench cheating was an unknown vice between us; that
is to say, neither party would deliberately
smuggle on to the return of trench stores
handed over a dozen picks or shovels that
could not readily be accounted for.

We felt a genuine regret at quitting our humble quarters, because we had been at so many pains to make them habitable and replete with as many comforts as they were capable of sustaining. And we sorrowed that no longer, except as guests, would we light our " Little Kitcheners " in *Mulviross Villa*. Emancipated once more from the clogging life of the trenches, we marched off by companies at 9.35 p.m., fortunately without incurring a single casualty. Everything was favourable to the changing-over. The night was calm and a full moon blazed down on the ripe fields of corn. It did not seem like war. The only intimation of the death-grip of the trenches was the splutter of the machine guns and, until we were well away from the scene, the occasional frrrt of a spent ball. By midnight we were swinging along the Grand National, fatigued but cheery, and quite prepared to accept such rest for mind and body as the billeting officer and his myrmidons saw fit to provide for us.

We woke up the following morning to find ourselves in the delightful little village of

Bresle, situated in the dip of a rich countryside. Supporting a population of only 150, it satisfied all our ideals of rest and seclusion. There was no traffic to disturb the attention unduly. It harboured only a few inhabitants, mainly women and children, although a few soldiers on leave were to be seen tilling their fields. And here was a very remarkable thing and worthy of copy, the extreme intensity of cultivation. Every available ounce was utilised. The fertility of steep hillsides was stimulated by the artifice of terracing them. We spent those happy, tranquil days in restful abandon by the cornfields. Disburdened, we gave ourselves up to innocent relaxation. Discord and *brouillerie* were for the morrow. No longer impounded within the prison house of the trenches, we resumed the interrupted current of our freedom. The weather was tolerant. Nay, the warm airs were full of that warm delicacy of late summer which gratifies the senses while it restores the tone of the body. I was billeted along with the remaining officers of " D " Company in one of the better-class houses, of which there were indeed few, with a garden all red with geraniums and festooned with creeping vines, and in the corner there was a seat to which the approach was so narrow that we laughingly called any attempt to reach it, "forcing the Dardanelles." Alas! how few are now alive to appreciate the allusion. Two of us alone remain of that happy brotherhood, and, when we cast back our minds, perhaps we smile a little at some amusing recollection; we smile, and then we say: "But the others——!" And we smile no longer.

Madame was so very kindly disposed towards us. And her daughters too, who were married, and had a little brewery where a cooling draught of beer was invariably offered to us when, hot and dusty with the day's march, we returned from the line. Indeed, all the good people of Bresle denied themselves of a multitude of comforts in order that the soldiers might not go wanting. During this brief respite the hours were not given over entirely to empty and unprofitable inactivity. The needs of the trenches still called for numbers of willing labourers.

PILGRIMS IN PICARDY

The others were exercised daily in the arts of drill and discipline. All this time the battalion was supplying its working parties, but till the present moment they concerned me not at all. Each working party was always under the direction of an officer of the Royal Engineers, and when the gang commander reported to this officer he was shown his task and given his instructions. It fell to my lot to have charge of one of four gangs to whom were entrusted the duties of digging a new communication trench in the sloping ground between Bécourt and Albert. Night was the only time suitable for the accomplishment of this task. A bright moon shone down, and when we had collected our tools from the R.E. dump at Albert, and picked our way perilously through the tangles of barbed wire half hidden in the grass, the soft rays, filtered through a filigree of almost invisible cloud, gleamed on the shovels. The light that favoured our craft did not, however, discover the craftsmen to the enemy. And before 1 a.m. a trench 200 yards long, and dug uniformly to a depth of six feet, had been completed, to be extended on successive nights by further parties encouraged in the hope that hostile interference would not annul their efforts.

In the fullness of time, when our bodies were refreshed and our minds tranquillised by rest, we quitted the calm seclusion of Bresle and Laviéville and entered upon another period of anxious inactivity in the same trenches vacated on the 21st. The discretionary powers vested in ———'s office of adjutant to the battalion overruled the original reluctance of the companies to alter their relative positions. In this way I no longer occupied *Mulviross Villa*, but another of much less pretentious design called *Villa Albert*, situated at a point where the main communication trench, Aberdeen Avenue (or, at an earlier date, the Boyau Thalweg) debouched upon the firing line. For the first four days meteorological conditions determined to a large extent the volume and intensity of fire. At no time did it exceed the normal measure of aggressiveness. Yet absolute tranquillity did not reign over the disturbed and contested ground. The nervousness conspicuous in the attitude of the enemy was without doubt a *reflected* nervousness. For on either side of him the powder magazines of violence were fiercely ablaze. Both at La Boisselle and at Fricourt the earth hardly ceased to tremble from the eruptive upheaval of the mines. A shudder seemed to be passing continually between the two places. The Germans, too, were concentrating their energies on the construction of a wide redoubt immediately opposite our sector, whose value was only too clearly revealed when light trench mortar bombs began to rain down upon a corner that hitherto had been favoured by an agreeable immunity from disturbance. From our point of view the times were anxious, because there were entrusted to our hands to be moulded to the necessities of the trenches the first drafts of K1. Proud, indeed, did we feel in our office of instructors. It was a rare compliment to a Territorial Division. Then, on September 12th, we were relieved by the 6th Seaforths. The release from trench duty was indeed accepted with pleasure, not so much because the nerves had been adversely affected in the interval, but because the scarcity of water had made this bohemianism too extreme. The night was favourable for the relief, congestion was avoided, and the whole operation carried out without a casualty. At 3.15 a.m. we lay down to sleep at Laviéville.

Dawn had not yet begun to dissipate the fogs lying heavily in the folds of the ground when we re-entered Laviéville. The march from the firing line was not in itself a sufficient cause for the fatigue that manifested itself in the dragging limbs and heavy eyes. But the unhygienic conditions, the want of a proper toilet, and the uncharitable weather combined to provoke a distress which the toil of marching accentuated. In a short time each man had flung himself down on the patch of straw that served as his bed and surrendered his tired body into the sweet captivity of sleep. Refreshed at length by a rest such as we had not known for many days, and having ministered with worthy diligence to the needs of our outward persons, there still remained the duty of composing the mind, " in silence and unswerving," to face dangers of war. The day was clear—so clear that the tragic magnificence of the shattered basilica of Albert shone in the full glory of noon. There were white streaks of chalk on the distant uplands. These were the trenches. Behind us, almost hidden in apple trees, lay the deserted church of Laviéville. The *curé* was away fighting as a soldier-priest. Our own church parade was short and simple, befitting such a conventicle as this. The General attended with his aide-de-camp. After the introductory psalm the Colonel read the lesson, and then the padre spoke on the subject of " True Courage." In times of stress and trial, he pointed out the only way to acquire that almost terrible calmness in action, that " making firm the shuddering breath." After the National Anthem had been sung the men dispersed, some to clean their soiled linen, others to write to the loved ones at home that they were still " in the pink," while in our own happy circle we were welcoming back to our midst three officers incapacitated at Festubert, but now recovered.

The excessive heat of these days made all

exercises more than usually strenuous. Somewhat to our surprise these were abruptly terminated on the 16th, when sudden orders were issued to take over a new part of the line. We succeeded a very composite body of men, comprising Jats, Sikhs, and King's Dragoon Guards. We found the Indian sitting in his little bay of trench awaiting bullet or bomb with impassive and uncanny calm. It was Kismet. His immense puggaree looked quite out of proportion with his attenuated legs. His rough beard gave him an appearance of unnatural ferocity. His claw-like fingers seemed to be twitching to grip the resilient flesh of an enemy throat. The inflexibility of his diet—for the Indian lives almost exclusively on rice and chupatties—was repulsive to our minds. He looked dignified and self-satisfied, but, my faith! he had courage. Our guides, after losing themselves repeatedly and irritating our fellows beyond endurance, finally succeeded in extricating themselves and the tangled columns, and late at night my battalion posted its sentries without incident.

The sector into which we were now thrust

was designed "G 1." It was roughly the segment of a circle of which the centre was the village of Authuille. The boundary radii were Campbell Avenue and Thiepval Avenue. The former, so-called after our Brigadier-General, followed the course of the road that inclined from Authuille to Ovillers. The other avenue led direct to Thiepval of evil fame, until the bulwark of our front line rudely cut it short at a point where a solitary telegraph pole shot up out of an immense wilderness of weeds. Within this circumscribed area were many excellent trenches and a few on which a malevolent influence seemed continually to rest. The shelters as they existed in those days were designed to withstand only the most moderate shelling, but they fulfilled all our expectations, and *Patiala*, where a captain and myself sought harbourage, sleeping as well as the confining limits permitted, was a distinct improvement on all our past possessions. Perhaps he will forgive me the admission that it *was* a tight fit for two.

The night 16/17 proved to be tolerably quiet; the Indians melted out of the line;

the silence with which our own troops took over lulled the suspicion of a wary enemy; and the expectation of a lively cannonade was not realised. Hurried out of good billets at a time when the distractions of rest were doubly gratifying, urged to share again the common danger, we were not insensible to the pleasures we were asked to forsake. But the blind devotion which makes the martyr forget all in the ecstasy of his exaltation, fortified us against murmurs. We had expected a severe shelling; we found tranquillity. We had fears of a factious and refractory garrison in the line; but we relieved a garrison amongst whom there was not one bickering or dissentient voice.

And indeed there was little enough cause for dissatisfaction. The trenches were tolerably good; the dug-outs plentiful; the defences sound. The commissariat worked admirably. Supplies, indeed, were in profusion rather than the reverse. The weather was so calm and agreeable that one evening, during a temporary lull, a German brought out his violin, playing one of those touching volkslieder which affected me almost to tears.

He was a musician of many moods. If the night were quiet and still, he favoured Grieg. If his comrades, too ribald, rallied him to play something in a more popular vein, he gave them a valse of Waldteufel. When they were lovesick, he intoxicated them with a few bars of Liszt.

During these nights we worked hard at our entrenchments, taking full advantage of the favourable conditions. On the 19th the Germans did not, as was their wont, dispute our right to improve our trenches. And for the very good reason that they were conspiring to improve their own. The night was tranquil; the wind but a whisper; the sky lustrous with stars. Across No Man's Land drifted the metallic clank of iron-shod mallets and the dulled grind of shovels in the chalk. We found the Germans, as we have always found them, industrious and painstaking. No labour was thought too hard, no sacrifice too terrible, if it could prolong a sentry's life or render a dug-out more enduring. They sweated, not so much on their own behalf but for the benefit of future garrisons. Their toils were not momentary whims, nor mere exercises for idlers; nor wholly punishments inflicted on those who had incurred the displeasure of the authorities. Prisoners guilty of some offence against military law were indeed impressed into such service. To them probably fell the more perilous undertakings. But the marvellous earthworks from which the defenders could, after the most intense bombardment, emerge dangerous and defiant, from which they could parry the most powerful thrust, into whose galleries they could retire and exist independent of supplies until their own stores became exhausted, must surely have been due to the collective energy, industry, and zeal of the German soldiery.

To counteract that inestimable spirit we had to oppose not only a confidence in our ultimate power to break it down but a present diligence to humble and mortify it. We shelled the labourers. We dismantled their emplacements with well-aimed shots. We tore down their defences, scattered their sand-bags, and laid their defences in ruins. But as often as we destroyed, they rebuilt. As often as we challenged, they replied.

PILGRIMS IN PICARDY

We razed Thiepval to the ground; they fired salvos over Authuille. We raked the château; and they retaliated on the carriage drive. But although they fenced and parried, they could not hope in the end to withstand the stubborn opposition already making itself manifest in our ranks. The reason of their increasing aggressiveness may, perhaps, be summed up in the words of Von der Goltz in that admirable book of his on *The Conduct of War*: "He who thinks only of parrying can at best avert his own defeat. The result for him is a negative one. He simply frustrates the purpose of his adversary."

During the afternoon of the 19th the enemy, inconsiderately casting about to annoy us, bombarded our trenches with liberal salvos of whizz-bangs and trench mortars. But our retaliation proved so effective that, after all had quietened down, the Germans were heard cursing with great energy. It was not unlikely that they had suspicions of our relief, with which, by a stroke of good fortune, their bombardment did not coincide. At midnight the battalion was clear of the front line. "D" Company had been allotted a reserve trench, but could not occupy it till dawn. In the meantime it went to rest in a collection of wicker hutments built on the ground that sloped down steeply to the River Ancre, which here broadened out into a considerable marsh. These hutments, which went by the collective name of Tiger Town, were infested by rats bold even to temerity and in numbers uncountable.

At dawn all were in their new quarters, one platoon of "D" Company having been detailed to defend a particular trench in the outer defences of Authuille, the other three dwelling as comfortably as was possible in the circumstances by the roadside, along which was strung a great number of rough shelters from the cemetery to the church. The houses of Authuille presented a very fair picture of the devastation of war, but at this time the destruction was not irreparable. My own dug-out indeed had sorry pretensions to prosperity, for the walls that remained upright were pocked by rifle balls and shell splinters. Here we laid down our packs, assumed a proprietary interest over the " grounds," and defied the weather and the Hun to do his respective worst. The other officers lived in a deserted estaminet, " Au Rendez-Vous des Chasseurs," on Wick Road. Of all the houses in the district this seemed to have suffered the least. We had a kitchen appointed entirely to our taste, and a very tolerable cook. The rooms were spacious and nearly intact. An upper window yielded a delightful panoramic view of the fighting front, and under the *mansardes* there was a constant hum of bees, which would still be making honey had not a brother officer, whom a sweet tooth rendered importunate, one morning descended upon our premises and raided the store.

Till September 29th all was normal. The disturbance at Loos was here apparent in a heavy and reciprocal shelling, not sufficient to cause apprehension. Authuille, being a good subject for exploration, in our lost moments we found it diverting enough to steal through the ruins and try to reconstruct the lives of the inhabitants. One day I tried to get some trout from the Ancre, but my bomb was defective and fell into the water with a splash, and raised no more disturbance than a little geyser of mud.

At 8 p.m. on the 30th we were relieved by the 5th Seaforths, which again gave us the opportunity of showing, in a manner not unpleasing to both, the collective affection of the unit. Our road, or rather beaten track, lay through a large wood, the Bois d'Aveluy, just beginning to scatter its leaves and to make the gunners uneasy about their camouflage. As a result of the recent heavy rains and the constant passage of pack-mules, the roads, never strong and particularly unsuited to meet the exigencies of war, even although they were reinforced by timber logs and metal, were ploughed into deep furrows of mud. At 11 p.m., in Martinsart, in a village not yet vacated by the inhabitants, we began another short term of rest.

Rest! We knew how illusory was the prospect of it. From a regular programme of fatigues we did not once deviate. Whatever relaxation was allowed to our over-spent bodies was regulated by a wise and sparing

THIEPVAL CHÂTEAU BEFORE THE WAR

hand; for prolonged leisure, not less than physical exhaustion, tended to enfeeble us. Work ranged from trench-repairing at Albert to route marches, with their incidental tactical problems to be worked out. These were pursued despite the trying climatic changes, which one day favoured us with bright and glorious sunshine and next day drenched us to the skin.

On the 9th an advance party was sent down from rest billets to take over from the 6th Argyll and Sutherlands the sector known as "G 2," confronting the village of Thiepval. Here we clung precariously to the narrow edge of the rising ground that inclined towards Bapaume. Behind us, cutting off our retreat, the River Ancre, broad and sluggish, flowed on to add its waters to the volume of the Somme. From the sector which we occupied in September we were separated by Thiepval Avenue. The outline of "G 2" conformed to the trace of the carriage drive that once served the château, the peculiar feature of the sector being the formation of two salients, called respectively North and South Salient. From each of these a well-defined sap ran out, Hammerhead and Maison Grise. And intermediately we found a tortuous passage following an oblique course to a lozenge clump of trees in the centre of the drive, which suggested its name, Diamond Wood Sap. The nature of all the trench names pointed at once to the battalion which had first placed its alien foot in these French positions, and with a singular disregard for the appropriateness of the original titles, altered them to Sauchiehall Street, Greenock Avenue, Buchanan Avenue, Paisley Avenue, and so on.

On the day preceding our arrival a sudden and totally unexpected bombardment of trench mortars had burst upon the centre company. The South Salient was disrupted, and Worgan Street almost obliterated. A pretty avenue of trees, aligning itself by Sauchiehall Street, had bordered this now desolated section of trench. Before the avalanche of explosives fell upon it, it had not been without charm; but within a few hours a scorched and maimed skeleton of this avenue spread its ragged edges over the confusion and ruin around. Tattered pieces of kilt hung in tartan ribbons from the blackened trees. High up on the naked boughs fluttered the white bandages of the stretcher bearers.

No truer picture of contemporary trench life can be found than in the journals that record all its varied phases, the moods and manners of the soldiers, the hopes and despairs incidental to an existence of boundless toil under such grievous restraints. I therefore transcribe verbatim my diary of the succeeding few days.

"*October 12th.*—9 p.m. *Pegamata.* Not an arrow's length distant the Hun can be heard picking at his chalk. The human mole is burrowing in the tunnels of his tumulus, or he is deepening the floor of its approach, or he is strengthening its ramparts. Our own men have crept to their shelters to shiver themselves into sleep. They are mud-stained and tired, having worked hard all day. Except for the occasional baying of a German watch-dog, the sullen roar of a random gun, the " whup " of a bullet by the ear, there is an unnatural quiet. A slip of moon plunges suddenly out of the clouds, and the sentry, peering anxiously over the parapet, sees the pale glimmer of the wire, the rag of a château, and the opaque depth of wood. His scrutiny discloses nothing, but he teases the industrious Hun with a volley, as if he were personally malicious, slips another charger into his magazine, and lowers his head behind the sheltering sand-bags. But Fritz is still plodding bravely at his dug-out.

"*October 16th.*—3 p.m.—Simpson is dead! He was dangerously wounded two days ago by minenwerfer in the South Salient, and conveyed at once to hospital; but all efforts to save his brave young life were unavailing. We are a little stupefied by the news.

"*Midnight.*—An intense quiet has settled upon the contending forces. For the moment there is not even a rifle shot, and flares are few. Both sides have lost their initial sense of irritation. The emotion of surprise has gone. Sentries no longer with twitching nerves see phantom Germans crawling towards the wire. The scampering of a rat intensifies the silence. Now it whimpers like a human thing, a melancholy sound. The reliefs arrive and the watches are changed. The fresh sentries, muffled up in their great-coats, peer fixedly out into the gloom, appear satisfied, then settle down to their two hours of unwinking vigil. Soon it is again oppressively silent. "Le silence éternal de ces espaces infinis m'effraie."

"*October 17th.*—Word has just reached us of the death of Captain Forsyth, wounded at the same time as poor Simpson. Strong hopes were entertained of his recovery, but the old man's wounds were mortal, and shock precipitated if it did not encompass the end. The circumstances of his death are the more sad as he was about to return to Scotland with a captain in whom the burden of advancing years did not suffer the diminution of an exalted patriotism."

Our acquaintance with "G 2" sector was not confined to this one visit. We came to know the sector thoroughly, to understand its peculiar dangers, and to learn how best to avoid them. Time after time we relieved the 5th Seaforths, and our officers did not want anything better than to assemble in

Feyther's dug-out in Paisley Avenue, where with a few kindred souls, such as Daavid and Tosh and Stalker, we met the grim facts of war with a kind of light-hearted dalliance. But poor Tosh will never more convulse us with the adventures of Mackay's smoke-helmet, nor will Stalker the irrepressible break more lances in friendly jousts of wit. For they are both counted among the fallen.

"*October* 20*th*.—At 7.40 p.m. we returned to our old billets at Martinsart, very pleased to announce our arrival at *Madataf* by a dinner such as we had not known for weeks.

"*October* 25*th*.—Units of our Army Corps were inspected to-day by the King, the Prince of Wales, and President Poincaré. The review ground stretched over some undulating fields adjacent to Bresle. Here flew the Union Jack and the Tricolor combined as one flag. A bitter wind swept over the open as with chattering teeth and numbed fingers we waited for the royal car. There was a slight delay in the proceedings. We were all proud, impatient hearts. From a neighbouring bluff the stirring treble of the pipes and the rataplan of drums lessened the suspense.

About noon an equerry rode up. The King was near. There was a hurried marshalling and a final dressing of the troops. A bugle blew. The car drove up with a staff officer in attendance. The brigades presented arms. His Majesty advanced, dressed in khaki, as was the Prince, looking somewhat slight beside the blue-caped figure of the French President. There was no waiting now. We marched past the saluting base in column of platoons, and formed up in mass on the spur of rising ground not far from the royal entourage. When all was over the thunder of our cheers rolled and died away."

On November 4th preparations for an interchange of trenches were begun. In the readjusted scheme those companies which had last braved the dangers of the firing line returned to the comparative security of the village defences of Authuille. An interval of fine weather made for a rapid transition, and Paisley Avenue, which all morning had presented a scene of culinary activity, now became the dumping ground of the regimental impedimenta. At length the perspiring relief, on this occasion the 7th

Black Watch, arrived with much voluble and unrestrained wrath. We showed them over the trenches apologetically, scarce hiding the smile with which we greeted their approach, and strove to impress upon them that these quarters were a paragon of comfort to what we ourselves had taken over. It was always curious to note how invariably sceptical of improvements were any newcomers. The qualities attributed to the " last lot in " were never very flattering. Captain X. of the Gordons, even with the most persuasive eloquence and oily cunning, would never have been able to convince Captain Y. of the Black Watch that he had been strictly attentive to draining and revetting and sand-bagging and wiring and so forth. The arrival of a relief always postulated their scathing indictment of the forces they relieved.

We occupied the reserve trench of this gigantic *œs triplex*, working hard most of the day and sleeping all night without interruption. The platoons were scattered over a vast network. Mine, in particular, lay in the outer defences, access to which was both easy and safe, being accomplished by means of a well-constructed communication trench. We messed daily in the remains of a house belonging to the widow of a M. Leseurre, a bibliophile, cousin of the French composer and critic, Camille Saint-Saens, and a personal friend of the Parisian novelist Gyp. In a cupboard I brought to light a good selection of books, notably Thiers' *French Revolution.* These and a few Zolaesque novels helped to while away the tedium of the trenches. Here I picked up out of the gutter a copy of Saint-Saens' poems, with this autograph on the fly-leaf: " A mon cher cousin et ami, Leseurre. C. Saint-Saens. 1893." M. Leseurre seemed to have been a man of comprehensive tastes in literature in whom the critical faculty was developed to an advanced degree. This was indicated by his papers, which I collected and stored away, hoping thus to save them from vandalism and extinction.

The main road to Thiepval passed by our cottage. Here was a wayside chapel and the beginnings of a trench. The weather-cock on the chapel still swung to the winds.

PILGRIMS IN PICARDY

Two hundred yards up this trench was *Hamelin,* presiding over a little township of dug-outs, the *mairie* of a Lilliput commune. It was commodious and well built, roofed with corrugated iron and bricks and protected from above by a loop-holed barbican. A close-fitting door defended us from draughts; a window admitted light; an improvised stove, whose chimney found a ready, if rough, exit by the window, gave us warmth sufficient for our needs. The outhouses of Widow Leseurre supplied us with fuel eked out by a sackful of coke. Our table had obviously been commandeered from the village, and also the chairs, including a wicker arm-chair, broken up one day in a time of dire necessity. A flourishing community of rats suggested the name *Hamelin* for our dug-out. Rats without number and of all sizes. The plague here existed in its most virulent and repulsive form. To leave a few scraps on my table was to make it the casino of ratland. Nightly visitations latterly blunted our feelings, until the pests took to playing with the *Scotsman* and tugging its gnawed remains out of sight.

Loss of food we could endure, but loss of sleep was intolerable. A grand old patriarch was their leader. He had his home above my pallet, and came out at dusk with much whimpering and pattering. Ultimately I laid him low. When he met his death he was celebrating a festival on a packet of chocolates and a tin of *café au lait*. In this pogrom perished with him five of his confederates, well fed with carrion.

On November 17th we were relieved by the 4th Lancashire Regiment and the 6th Scottish Rifles, of the 154th Brigade. I left in advance of the battalion. Avoiding the short route over the ridge to Bouzincourt, now deeply rutted by artillery and transport wagons, I chose a longer and more circuitous road by Englebelmer. An error of judgment deflected me from my course, which caused me some inconvenience and no little annoyance, as it was dusk when I arrived and snow had begun to fall. In default of better lodgings we were billeted in an empty house of Hénencourt, but before we settled down we ordered a good meal in the estaminet of the main street, the estaminet "Au Petit

Caporal." I strongly advise any visitor to this village to call and ask for mutton cutlets. They will delight his heart. Let him also ask for Epernay, for the *cuvée* is above reproach. The hospitable Picard family of this inn included a grandam, on whom the asperities of advancing age had not yet begun to make an impression. She sat in her corner chair, like a queen, very calm and dignified. Her regal manners and pleasing countenance, combined with a natural affability, were touching and striking proofs of a well-ordered household. Madame prepared our cutlets while Mademoiselle, whose unaffected simplicity and distinguished mien proclaimed her at once a charming kitchen-adjutant, was pleased to serve us.

We transferred our personal effects to a more comfortable billet next morning, under the hospitable roof of Devarguet-Gosselin at the estaminet " A L'Alliance Franco-Russe." We were lodged in an upper chamber, where slept but a few weeks previously (so Madame said) " Le commandant McMillan . . . très gentil homme." Many other officers were our mutual acquaintances. She managed to pronounce their names well, apologising for any mistake with a singular felicity of phrase. And who could have the heart to laugh if the name of Rutherford presented difficulties too foreign for her tongue?

We left Hénencourt at 10 o'clock, with an additional supply of apparel, for the weather was now assuming a more threatening aspect. The soft genial skies had disappeared, and we found no longer a Picardy of mellowing orchards and charming plains, but a Picardy clad in the cerements of a dead autumn. A sharp frost held the countryside fast in its grip. On the way to Millencourt we passed two cemeteries, a little neglected on account of the dearth of labour. In respect of its puzzling streets and quaint little byways, Millencourt was not dissimilar to the village we had just left behind us. We skirted the northern extremity of Albert, bearing past the station and the Swedish vice-consulate. The road now turned abruptly to the left and followed a natural course through a well-defined valley. The rains had swollen the marshes of the Ancre, and broad sheets of water now covered the reeds. Fair to look upon and fringed with meadows of perennial green, the tiny waves, breaking among the reeds, rippled over the countless graves of German dead.

Three kilometres beyond Albert we entered Aveluy, which brought us immediately behind our entrenchments. A narrow culvert spanned the river. In front rose a steep and irregular escarpment, whose frowning face looked over a scene of great activity. Beside a wayside Calvary were ration dumps, and R.E. stores, and smithies, and an advanced kiosk of the Expeditionary Force Canteen. A bridle-path led over a col, and brought us to the beginning of a long communication trench which it was wise to traverse.

Our new trenches, designated " F 1 " subsector, spread fanwise over a saddle of rising ground, disappearing on the northern extremity into Authuille Wood, which was of considerable size. In some parts the calcareous nature of the soil endowed the trenches with a greater degree of permanency than usually obtained. But the large proportion of heavy brown loam in the remainder of the sector made the labour of our hands fugitive and insecure. The earth, becoming saturated and heavy, invariably collapsed on the least provocation, and the detritus collecting on the floor of the trenches in wet weather formed a glutinous compound through which it was almost impossible to walk. The denomination of these trenches had been entrusted to units of the 154th Brigade, and it was therefore common to find ourselves struggling from Post Donney to Palatine, or to Fishergate, or labouring in the quagmires of John o' Gaunt Street. The battalion frontage was extensive, approximating a mile in length. From its highest point, opposite Ovillers, a magnificent enfilading view disclosed the wreckage of La Boisselle. It seemed as if a giant slumbering in the bowels of the earth had awaked and heaved his immense shoulders. A series of accidents combined with the inclemency of the weather had devastated many of our dug-outs and impaired the remainder. We elected therefore to sleep in a shelter, neither impervious to water nor proof against shells. It was hoped that the frost would continue, but the expanded earth burst the gabions. A heavy mist now began to spread its dense white folds around the spine of rising ground. The frost relaxed and the air became humid.

The trenches had been weathered to such an extent, both by exposure to the elemental infelicities and by their subjection to hostile shelling, that it was almost a superhuman effort to patrol in one day the whole extent of line. It was impossible, for instance, to combine the duties of examining the battalion bomb-stores and attend to the normal business of the platoon. These, indeed, were the particular tasks entrusted to my care, but I was fortunate in possessing a bombing sergeant whose competence was always above reproach. These vicarious duties he always performed so thoroughly and conscientiously that at no time did I find my confidence misplaced. The enemy was separated from us at an average distance of 200 yards. He was not methodically aggressive. As a rule the nights passed tranquilly. A few light shells did indeed explode close by, but these

LA BOISSELLE

were haphazard and caused us no damage, and between dusk and midnight a desultory firing was usually sustained. Dawn often reacted on both sides, the customary stand-to being responsible for a slight increase in the volume of fire. My duty log for the period recorded nothing save a great deal of enemy vehicular traffic; but my hours of off-duty were marked by heavy bombardments on the left, on what appeared to be a scrofulous bald acclivity seamed with innumerable trenches. We were particularly on our guard, therefore, lest the Germans should practise the shallow stratagem of launching an attack on one part of the line by diverting the attention to another.

It was under such circumstances that I received my first warrant for short leave. I left shortly after midday on the 24th, with the Major's benedictions and the good-humoured banterings of the mess, enjoined to beware, while exposed to far greater dangers than those of the firing line, the febrile impetuosity of youth.

Part II—May to November 1916

VII   MINES AND MISERIES

ON May 18th, the clear notes of réveillé roused us up at 5 a.m., to view with an impatient expectation the novelty of our present case; and having filched some soap from the neighbouring mess, without accounting it a mean felony or a piece of unconscionable impropriety (for our valises had not yet arrived from the station), we drew some water and effaced all the traces of recent travel, the more conformably to observe the ritual of reporting. The hutments of Ripon here gave place to apparently endless lines of bell-tents, dressed regularly on the white sandy dunes. There appeared to be an uncommonly large number of wooden erections, an admixture in most respects comprising Y.M.C.A. huts, canteens, officers' messes, orderly rooms, and housing of a like nature, to which the eye, roving over the illimitable resources, gradually grew accustomed. We had been accommodated temporarily in some empty tents in the lines of the 32nd Divisional Depot, grateful for the privilege but incontinently savage that absence of our baggage discounted the convenience of the arrangement. Our guests being strictly rationed could not extend to us a warmer welcome than that of an encouraging word of advice, which was indeed offered without the usual exhibition of diffidence, and therefore made us eager to respect the slenderness of their board.

About 8 o'clock, famished after such a long fast, I strolled into Étaples in order to find a meal, and in very truth this quaint little town was pleasantly supplied with a number of charming restaurants, as peculiar in their appearance as their dinners were *recherché*. I found that two restaurants were set apart for the use of officers, the Café des Voyageurs near the station, and the Café Loos in the interior of the town. I have dined in both, and on each occasion have come away satisfied that, howsoever controlled by a wise and provident economy, these establishments can appease the most violent hunger at prices of great moderation. And, mark you, the landlords are descended from those rapacious *aubergistes* whom Smollett, travelling in the year 1763 in these very parts, described as the most villainous robbers, destitute of every good feeling and as palpable in their impositions as they were illiberal in their terms. But where poor consumptive Smollett was " served with the appearance of the most mortifying indifference at the very time they were laying schemes for fleecing him of his money," we experienced complaisance instead of churlishness, assiduous attention instead of indifference, courtesy instead of insolence, and moderation instead of extortion.

I breakfasted at the Café des Voyageurs, as it was conveniently near the camp and I was not minded to travel far afield till I had satisfied the ragings of my appetite. Even at this early hour the little tables outside were taken by travellers enjoying their *petit déjeuner* in the genial sunshine. Reinforcement officers wearing dark blue gorgets toned down the dash of red affected by the Staff, and a few French officers dressed in light blue tunics lessened the sombreness of the prevailing khaki. At noon I reported to the O.C. Reinforcements, and was immediately directed to my battalion lines, but, as it was now too late to participate in the particular functions of the day and the adjutant of the battalion proved not too *exigeant*, I was persuaded to join a party to Paris-Plage. The weather was now scorchingly hot, and the heat reflected by the blazing sands considerably aggravated. The intemperate heat of the summer and the glare of the dunes unmitigated by verdure provoked a distaste of walking abroad in the daytime, even with the alluring prospect of a burnished sheet of sea sweeping up to the esplanade of Paris-Plage, and the umbrageous retreats of Le Touquet intervening. To the end, therefore, that travellers from Paris, resorting for the benefit of their health to the generous breezes of the coast, may not first be committed to the painful necessity of proceeding on foot from Étaples to their destination, tramcars, with open sides to admit a continuous current of fresh air, have been introduced. On the way to Paris-Plage we passed through the woods of Le Touquet, intersected everywhere by little bypaths where wounded French soldiers were hobbling about. Soon, however, we entered the domain of houses, and quite suddenly came upon a steep incline, whereon were perched châlets of fanciful and grotesque architecture, spires and turrets all fantastically reaching up and gleaming in their warm colourings.

After drinking a refreshing brew of tea at the Chat Bleu, where some delicious pastries were to be had for a sum very inconsiderable having in view the fact that they were made in an obscure little house in Étaples, we first gratified Miller's desire to procure for the mess some lily of the valley which, we were assured, had been picked up wild in the forest of Fontainebleau, and then followed a bridle-path homewards through woods of poplar and fir, the latter covering a hill capped by an outlook tower from which could be seen an extensive panorama stretching away for miles. The erection of this tower had been conceived with some subtlety, and executed in such a manner as to exclude from the view too great a multitude of extraneous objects and to permit the eye only to rest upon a soft receding cushion of trees. In the distance the multi-coloured châlets peeped out of the prevailing green. The light tints, melting into a yellowish brown, mingled exquisitely with the gold of the sands and the shimmering silver of the sea. Behind the tower the huddling tree-tops sloped gently towards the River Canche. By night everything was dead calm and the air hot and oppressive. Lying in my tent I listened to the nightingales singing in the woods and the frogs cree-cree-creeing, till, drowsed with sleep, I composed myself and sank into unconsciousness.

On May 21st a draft was paraded for the front, of which I, as the senior officer reporting, was put in command. Most of the men were rejoining my own unit, but a few artillerists were added to complete the draft. On our departure the Colonel spoke a few encouraging words, and upon bidding us God speed the padre prayed while the train was getting up steam, committing us in his earnest valediction to the care of a Supreme Being Who, while He encouraged the oppressed

MINES AND MISERIES

and strengthened the weary, could mortify the oppressor and subdue the strong. With these words of hope ringing in our ears we began our journey towards railhead, which an undue familiarity would have rendered uninteresting, had not a stimulant been required to defend the mind from the attacks of ennui. The slowness of our travelling would have drawn a eulogium from Fabius Cunctator himself were he resurrected from his Roman clay. It must not be thought, however, that speedy transit is always accounted superior to protracted locomotion; for there are certain times when deliberation rather than haste, and pleasant interruptions rather than precipitancy, seasonably propitiate the mind and incite the imagination to a fuller appraisement of rural beauties.)

For the space of two hours we traversed the most diversified country scenery, running out of wide stretches, where the crops were standing two feet high, into quaint clusters of houses with walls of glaring white plaster and red roofs, and, leaving these in the dusty distance, into the precincts of green paddocks and noble chases. There were a few marshes, where the frogs could be heard croaking with monotonous reiteration.

At six in the evening we ran into the station of Abbeville, where we detrained at the military siding, but the hard roads were so granulated by traffic that at every step we took the finest of dust particles rose up in clouds, irritating our throats, titillating our nostrils, and chafing our eyes. Having eight hours to while away in Abbeville we tried our practised blandishments on the R.T.O., who readily supplied us with a passport into the town, a favour for which we were abundantly grateful, and which we put into resolution immediately by ordering dinner at the Hôtel de la Gare.

At 7.30 the succeeding morning we detrained at Aubigny, railhead to the Vimy sector, and marched to Thilloy, where billets were allocated for the night. Active campaigning had already rendered me insensible to the finer susceptibilities, and as the hospitality of the A.S.C. had been extended to me, I took the precaution of studiously avoiding food in my billet lest nausea should engender an indisposition which was peculiarly rife at this time. During the night the activity of the artillery roused me repeatedly. I stirred constantly in my sleep, tumbling and tossing, and once awoke in a profuse sweat after having visualised in an impalpable but dreadful nightmare the hurricane attack which had lately deprived us of the northern spur of Vimy Ridge.

Next day I found my battalion transport at Bray, a delightful little village, secluded in a wooded depression and watered by the River Scarpe, here very narrow. With regard to situation nothing could be more agreeable, and surprise overcame me when I learned that large numbers of the population, terrified of the menace of the guns, had taken refuge in a quieter zone. By the side of the stream I discovered a tent ideally situated, where the rippling of the water mingled with the soughing of the trees. Thus the charm of nature tempered the afflictions with which man lancinated the feelings of his fellow creature; for surely there is no person living so obtuse in sensibility but is

MINES AND MISERIES

grieved and dejected by the horrors of war. A steep ridge separated us from the fighting lines. On the left of this ridge a misshapen and spectral tower reared its crumbling remains, which in my eyes were more comely and sublime because they were the visible expression of suffering. This grotesque ruin was none other than the famous Mont St. Eloi.

All day long the artillery continued heavily engaged. The roar of the cannon suffered no diminution. Indeed, the clamour of the guns increased as the approaching gloom made attack or counter-attack a contingency to be watched and measured. As night advanced the artillery action on the left became more and more intense, and the brilliance of the spectacle was proportionate to the violence of the guns. Lights likened to starry waterfalls blazed down on the devouring elements of war. Shells bursting high in the air emitted sudden tongues of flame. The shock of the high explosive seemed almost to penetrate to Bray.

It was three o'clock in the afternoon that I entered the first communication trench (for

MINES AND MISERIES

my battalion was then holding a portion of the line), and not till two and a half hours later, after weary and incessant walking, did I reach head-quarters. From this may be judged the enormity of the trench system, the resource, industry, and patience necessary to construct and repair it, and the devotion of the gallant *bleuets* who gave even their lives to render it impregnable. To whom did we owe all these safe avenues? There was evidence that cried to Heaven in the litter of lost equipment, in the innumerable wooden crosses already spangled with the petals of the cornflower and poppy. More pathetic than these, a corroding Lebel was sticking out of the wet clay, a decaying bone still crooked round the trigger. Often a rustling of the grasses discovered a patch of fading blue tunic or a red fragment of some dead hero's culottes. One dared not dig overmuch, because the whole ground was a vast cemetery and every closed-up dug-out a tomb. In the centre of all, the town of Neuville St. Vaast lay flattened into dust.

I rejoined my old company, " D," in the *Palais Caverne*, near the Rocade, a dug-out very commodious and deep, and so retired from the sunlight that candles had to be kept burning night and day.

Our tenure of the trenches from May 24th till the 27th was not signalised by any special occurrence, if we omit the usual battering of trench mortars and aerial torpedoes, which indeed came to be regarded, in consort with the hidden terror of the mine, as the *bête noire* of the Labyrinth. At the end of this period I left the trenches early in the morning in order to take over billets in Marœuil. The officers were billeted in a very tolerable house, called, for the sake of convenience, the *Little Château*, in Seaforth Street, in one wing of which lived the owners, two kindly disposed ladies of the name of Saison-Champagne. They were a much-travelled people, whose adventures embraced intimacies at the court of the Tsar Ferdinand of Bulgaria. They spoke with rapture of the Passion Play at Oberammergau, and never tired of relating amusing experiences of their voyages, mixing inconsequential details of travels at Toledo with a diary of devotions at

MONT ST. ELOI

Jerusalem, and making us follow with breathless rapidity in excursions to Constantinople and Egypt and the East.

But our stay at Marœuil terminated all too soon, and on the last day of the month it behoved us to bid good-bye to our charming friends at the château. They seemed very sad at our parting. When would we come back again? Would we have some honey liqueurs? And the marguerites, they were growing only that we might pluck them. And with a sigh that was half whimsical and half sincere, we left behind us the heavy scent of the flowers, the hum of the bees, and the mystery of the fountain that plashed no longer over the goldfishes.

In the evening, following the course of the sunken road between Ecurie and Neuville St. Vaast, we came to the Elbe Shelters, where we piled our scanty belongings and entered into occupation of an agreeable dugout, wherein, in the feeble light of a swinging candelabrum, we gave our minds to the study of the tactical situation before composing them to the tranquillity of the night. Hereafter I shall endeavour to give the reader an exact insight into the intimacies of trench life in this peculiar region, which differed so essentially from all other regions, by quoting my journal, the observance of which diverting entertainment undoubtedly helped to distract the mind from the horrible and the morbid.

"*June 1st.*—During the afternoon a heavy bombardment began on our left like the continuous rumble of thunder, but did not increase in intensity till darkness set in. We climbed a bank to watch the fire as it progressed. To the spectator at a distance the scene appeared terrible and grand. A thousand lightnings ran up and down the lines. Green, blue, and red fusees arched from either side. White Verey flares revealed nothing but rolling clouds of blinding dust and smoke. The noise was so great that the report of the heavy guns far to the rear reached us only as an indistinct *poop*. Doubts and hopes assailed us. My companion ventured his opinion that we were counter-attacking the lost spur of Vimy Ridge. At that moment a German machine gun began to sweep round, and a cloud of dust flew up from

MINES AND MISERIES

a neighbouring talus, driving us into security, where, the mails having arrived, we were no longer disposed to argument.

"*June 2nd.*—In the early hours of the morning the enemy exploded a camouflet, which is not to be confused with a mine. A camouflet has not for its primary object the destruction of parapets and the annihilation of men; it is intended to nullify an approaching mine by blowing in the gallery. There was no actual loss of life, but the dug-outs of the front line were badly shaken, and tremors of this sort were of so frequent occurrence that actual occupation of them often proved as risky as exposure in the open.

"*June 4th.—Villa Mignonette*, Rocade. A very effective raid resulted to-day in our obtaining valuable information concerning the identity and dispositions of the troops immediately opposing us. A succession of local raids is always the prologue to an offensive of any magnitude, because by this means enemy units are located with an amazing degree of accuracy. The intelligence so collated is vastly more important than the temporary damage inflicted upon the trenches or the loss of moral incurred by their occupants. To have learned that a frontage of twenty miles is thinly held by, let us say, the Wurtemburgers and the Saxons, is accounted more important by far than to possess the assurance that certain enemy elements have been destroyed and so many effectives put out of action. Wounds will heal and material damages can be repaired, but by the possession of their secrets we can take the measure of their opposition and inflict defeats.

"In the present instance, picked volunteers practised for the coup with zealous industry. The scene of their rehearsals was well behind the lines. The trenches to be raided were represented by tapes, accurately laid down and assiduously studied. All concerted to bring the forthcoming episode to a triumphant conclusion. The spirit of manly exercise was encouraged, and exceptional privileges were conceded in order to foster the offensive vigour, so that these sturdy men of Fifeshire and Perth, who were so soon to be tested in gallant enterprise,

MINES AND MISERIES

exempt from the fatigues of the line, devoted their bodies to physical and their minds to moral strength. At 4 o'clock of this very genial afternoon the watches of the troops directly and indirectly engaged were synchronised at Brigade Head-quarters. The French Brigade Staff had erected a charming street of dug-outs, and here in the sunshine the final preparations were made. These consisted mainly in arrangements for artillery support. The raiding party itself arrived at the Elbe shelters close after 6 o'clock, in fiery eagerness to go "over the top," and perhaps a little inclined to show my battalion, which was then tenanting the trenches, what the redoubtable Black Watch could do. It was a reasonable desire. In warfare egoism must count for more than altruism; it is the self-assertive who conquer.

"At 8.30 the artillery preparation began. All the guns possible were brought to bear on "N 1" sector. Guns of all calibres were rending the air with defiant detonation. Vimy was reverberant with the explosions of the heavies. The deep craters of the Labyrinth were being torn by trench mortars.

MINES AND MISERIES

The 18-pounders barked an incessant drum-fire. Throughout the turmoil came the deadly tattoo of machine guns. We waited with alert ears. The earth was quivering with the shock of detonated high explosive. Then a great trembling seized the ground. The sides of the dug-out swayed. Candles pitched forward, guttered a little, and went out. An immense column of earth and débris shot up from the German lines. Some of the débris fell into our own trenches. We had just sprung four mines, and the raiders, almost blinded by dust and confused by the terrible destruction, leapt over the parapet. At the first convulsion of the mines the guns lifted to the German support line and began to form what is known as a box-barrage, inside which, bent on their task of demolition and death, the Highlanders bombed dug-outs where the terrorised survivors of the enemy had fled for shelter. The casualties inflicted on the Germans were estimated at about forty killed, which a prisoner taken but a short time after confirmed.

" In addition to these heavy losses, three prisoners were brought back in the last stages of fear and collapse. At Brigade Headquarters they were assured that their fate would not be summary execution, and on that assurance supplied much valuable information. One of the prisoners was a huge Prussian of over six feet. His captor, a short-statured pygmy of five-feet-six, hauled him unresisting through the wire. The German was a fatalist, and seemed to be perfectly indifferent to the treatment he imagined would certainly be meted out to him. 'What could I do?' he said pathetically. 'I crawled out of my dug-out to find Scotchmen everywhere.'

"For this exploit Herd was awarded the much-coveted D.S.O., and never was decoration more justly earned. Besides instilling an irresistible élan into his men, he returned no less than three times to the scene of the raid in order to collect them, long after the scheduled time had expired. In sector "M 2" a new street named Herd Street commemorated the occasion, after the manner of the French. And how much more fittingly will Herd Street descend to posterity than The Pimple, the one recalling an incident where human endurance and courage were displayed, the other a mere descriptive title for a geographical excrescence.

"*June 7th.—Maison Blanche.*—For four days nothing could have induced us to quit this subterranean gallery save a 17-inch Skoda. Being detached from the battalion, which, although in support, was under the control of the battalion commanders in the line for reasons purely tactical, our position was anomalous. But the quasi-rest restored our flagging energies. We were still, however, as prisoners whose liberty is bounden with a wall—eating, sleeping, and refreshing our minds in the pestilential atmosphere of an underground cavern, and debarred from liberal exercise except such as we felt ourselves constrained to take in the open fields, where we were undoubtedly exposed to the observation of the foe.

"*June 8th.*—At length the moment arrived to sever our relations with the *White House*, and to complete the intricate process of relief which the readjustment of battalions rendered peculiar to this part of the line. The relief, timed for 6 o'clock, began with

MINES AND MISERIES

an occurrence of ill omen. The enemy must have been cognisant of the change, for we had scarcely been in occupation one hour when the Germans blew a camouflet, destroying one of our mine-shafts. This explosion was marked by an act of great personal sacrifice on the part of Corporal King, who gave his life in an heroic attempt to save that of a fellow soldier whom he saw slowly engulfed in the crumbling earth. My dug-out, situated in Rocade, announced on its wooden entrance the following words, remains of French occupation: '*Villa Mignonette,* Lieutenant Sapeurs Pionniers, Poste Secours.' I shared it with ——. It was an annexe to our old orderly room, since converted into a headquarters for the trench-mortar battery. It was a villainously confined apartment, but reasonably deep and safe.

"*June* 9*th.*—*Villa Mignonette,* Rocade, No. 1 Sector. 6–8 a.m.—Dawn was heralded by an intermittent shelling on the left. On our own side there was undertaken no destructive mortar fire, and the artillery lay quiescent. Times such as these gave the troops an opportunity of resting sorely tried nerves, or, if not passively resting, relieving the mind by work. As far as I myself was concerned much remained to be done in the removal of vast collections of French bombs, now useless, from the saps and the firing line, and in the rearrangement of our own stores. Company stores had to be constantly replenished. Harpur boxes had to be installed, and niches fashioned with care and security for their reception. ———, the brigade bombing officer, was the genius who conspired with that affection of his for anything explosive to make the grenadiers of the Highland Division incomparable.

"11 a.m.—A very heavy trench mortaring by the enemy induced for the time being a period of repose. These outbursts were spasmodic, and were expected to occur several times a day. Beyond damaging the trenches they availed little, and only inflicted an occasional casualty on an unfortunate sentry group.

"8.45 p.m.—A comical incident happened while we were at dinner in Sapper Shelters. We had just reached the stage of coffee and were lighting our Abdullas when the telephone bell rang violently. The adjutant sprang to the receiver. I forget what we were discussing; certainly nothing to do with the war; perhaps it was some story in the last number of *Punch*, or somebody's amours. The adjutant turned round excitedly to the mess with the startling announcement that 'D' Company reported Zeppelins passing overhead in a westerly direction. Everybody seized binoculars and rushed out to scan the sky. 'There it is,' shouted the Signals Officer. 'And another! Can't you see their shimmering bodies?' At that the F.O.O. dashed to the telephone and rang up his battery. Still more and more airships seemed to be moving out of the clouds into the patch of clear sky. 'Fleets of them!' murmured the adjutant. But we slipped quietly to our dug-out when we overheard the sentry say in a loud whisper to his comrades, 'They're a' daft, an' their eyesicht's no worth a preen. Fleyed at a puckle STARS!'

" One of the officers just back from leave dispelled from our minds all hopes of the safety of Kitchener. But he encouraged us by refuting all the unfortunate rumours that had been circulated about the fall of Verdun. Indeed, he cheered us with news of a fine French rally and the recapture of Fort Vaux, an elation toned down in its turn by the sense of an irreparable loss in the death of Kitchener.

"*June* 10*th*.—Dawn came with all those dull elements which are so often the prelude to a day of blistering heat. It did not come as usual with a burst of mortar fire. How frequently is the glory of morn made horrid by this blast of death! If we expected heat, however, it was denied us. Instead, very heavy rains descended, and at times hail showers and some thunder prevailed. This weather continued until late at night. One can scarce imagine to what an extremity the troops in the line were exposed. Their dug-outs had long since been deemed unsafe. By constant mining they had been rocked to this condition. Those in 'M 2' sector were particularly untrustworthy, and no troops were allowed to occupy them. To add to these discomforts the Germans continually challenged our superiority of fire by severe trench mortaring and salvos of ·77's. But

MINES AND MISERIES

the most dreaded nightmares of the Labyrinth were without doubt the mine and the camouflet. Their craters were lip to lip in No Man's Land. Our previous front line had been so disastrously cut up by a succession of great mines that it no longer existed as such. It was now held as an observation line. Sentry groups kept constant watch at the saps overlooking each crater. For a long time our mining was defensive, but gradually offensive mining became a more important part of operations. Each side, however, still succeeded in springing surprises on the other. Even now the sappers reported a mine under Claudot, and arrangements had to be made to cope with the possibility of its being exploded. These precautionary measures took the form of a readjustment of sentry groups, a new formation of machine guns to bear on the danger area, and a massing of bombs for the inevitable scramble in the crater. To meet this sudden crisis Bentata was almost depleted of its extensive stores. On the day we quitted the trenches for the quieter retreats of Marœuil, Claudot was tamped and ready."

VIII   IN THE WAKE OF THE PUSH

MARŒUIL remains in my memory as one of those charming French villages gallant in the blazonry of a summer sun. I can remember it even now, fanned by a breeze as soft as that of the Midi when the mistral is no longer blowing. The town dozed amid the poppy-red fields, now desolate. From Brunehaut Farm to the cemetery was a riot of red flowers. Within the town were gay orchards and gardens of fine splendour. Here the battalion was warmly received and excellently housed, head-quarters going into billets in the Little Château, by which name was known the " Cottage Notre Dame des Abeilles." At night there was the usual forgathering of officers in the most convenient estaminet. The only habitable room of the château of Gordon Street boasted a piano and a huge long table, which was of such grand dimensions as to bring to

IN THE WAKE OF THE PUSH

memory out of the storied past the ancestral halls of baronial France. It was truly a strange study of faces as the merry cycle of song rose to our lips : the pensive, hungering gaze of one who had listened to the deathless strains of " My Ain Wee Hoose " from the lips he might never touch; jovial and mellow of him who had sung " John Peel " at some academic carousal. We sang not in the offensive spirit of bravado, but in the spirit of gentle reminiscence—songs of the homeland that gloried in its beauty, songs of love that perpetuate the sweet surrender of women, songs of warfare on land and sea. Standing we sang the " Marseillaise," and then the equally beautiful " Brabançonne." Then, when we had toasted the Allies, somebody started " Auld Lang Syne," and, moved as by a common impulse, everybody joined hands, singing with such genuine fervour that there was not a heart but felt emotion.

But amid such innocent relaxation the war pursued its relentless course. Ere we had concluded our entertainment, the Germans had blown up the mine at Vissec, and the guns in consequence were hammering in strength. All this renewed activity put us on a footing of wary expectation. And when, on June 1st, we again took over the line, we felt ourselves to be on the eve of portentous discoveries. An officer, who had *carte blanche* to the whole line, usually presented the most interesting view of the current situation. He had discovered overnight large transport movement behind Thélus, which coincided with the divisional intelligence that a German Army Corps was being moved from our area. Probably the persistence of our raids and the extraordinary violence of our artillery inclined the enemy to the belief that a big offensive was impending. The shock of coming battle was certainly being felt here. Albert was generally thought to be the centre of our activities. When the bolt was to be launched remained as yet a profound secret. Hearing the guns thundering in the distance infected us with an expectation which could not be gratified by mere report.

But we were not the only party interested in the approaching struggle. The Germans, too, felt a stirring in the atmosphere and

IN THE WAKE OF THE PUSH

heard the whisperings of the storm. A sudden aerial nervousness became evident. The enemy increased their air patrols, to discover where our troops were being massed, and energetically tried to hamper our reconnaissances. They assumed a more offensive spirit. Perhaps they were trying to conceal some military movements from the prying eyes of our aviators; the attempt was unavailing. Perhaps they had orders to locate the precise frontage of attack; they failed. Each day large hostile formations crossed our lines, to be met and dispersed by our own machines. The innumerable encounters, however, were not always to our advantage, for at this time the redoubtable Fokker was at the zenith of its popularity. These well-contested duels were the necessary preliminaries to the great push slowly germinating in the south; losses we had to sustain ere the mastery of the air could be assured. And all the world knows how that mastery was made and maintained.

The hostile activity manifested in the air had a counterpart on land. The mind of the enemy as a whole, hitherto so disdainful and envenomed, became impregnated with doubt. Their obvious inability to plot the point of attack with accuracy rendered them peculiarly suspicious, so that they became nervous in their behaviour and intemperate in their use of " frustration fire." Mines began to be exploded injudiciously, which only succeeded in stirring up still more the unstable Doublemont. Bombs rained ineffectually on half-empty trenches. The artillery opened with sudden and sustained vigour, and then ceased as suddenly. Observation balloons sprang up where before the sky had been entirely innocent of them. On June 20th, a day of very clear visibility, eight of these monsters kept the enemy informed of all our movements, which inflamed us to fury on account of our expected relief. Till these were removed, therefore, relief had to be abandoned. At noon there was a welcome threat of rain, and the tireless eyes could no longer see. The dullness became a drizzle, and the work of exchange was instantly begun. At 4.35 battalion headquarters went to *Maison Blanche,* whose name alone remains in proud testimony to

IN THE WAKE OF THE PUSH

the fiery onslaught which on that bloody May 9th delivered the Labyrinth into the rightful hands of France.

The terrible gunfire on the right still continued without abatement. Sometimes it was scarcely audible; at other times the repercussion of sound was such as to daunt even the stoutest heart. And we debated among ourselves whether the Germans, rushing away troops to maintain the equipoise of the threatened front, would expose themselves here to the danger of unexpected surprise. But there was scarce a man who dared affirm that an enemy, as astute in strategy as he was courageous in the field, would suffer the lesion of weakness at any point to bring in its train decay and dissolution. For a morbid change in moral is a fatal affection to which an embarrassed army readily succumbs. Because the suspicion was rife that the enemy's forces garrisoning the Vimy sector had suffered a sensible diminution to counteract our overmatching numbers in the south, rumours began to circulate that we proposed to create a diversion on this front, and the arrival of fresh

IN THE WAKE OF THE PUSH

drafts lent all these rumours a semblance of colour. Our rifle strength was now augmented by two hundred men collected from all sources, an increase which proved to be common to all units.

At this juncture I fell ill of a trench fever, and was evacuated to the 2/1st Highland Field Ambulance at Haute Avesnes. Harassing work and perfidious weather conspired to undermine my health, and would have succeeded had not timely rest re-established it. It was now June 26th, and the guns were pounding in unprecedented fury. I remembered a day similar to this last year. We happened to be lying in Authuille, and in the north the gates of Loos were being hammered down. The sensation was the same—a feeling of eerie ecstasy, of exalted transport foretelling triumphs. We could imagine that torrential rain of death and the livid things enduring it. The tornado of battle now became real. A ceaseless muffled roar swelled to our ears. And we were exulting awfully. When would *our* time come ? That was the question—when ?

But the weather broke down, and the

IN THE WAKE OF THE PUSH

intensity of the guns died away. No news came through except the vaguest of rumours. And we were so impatient for news. Had the attack begun? Or was this merely a postponement? Nobody could tell. The Staff, if they knew, kept their lips well sealed.

Among the many reports circulating at this time was one of a divisional relief. It seemed clear at last that it was to be substantiated. For some time past it had been current in the trenches that the 60th Division was on its way to our relief, but a large amount of discredit was cast upon such news. So often had we been disillusioned! The actual arrival, however, of the division endorsed the common report. On the last day of June the 2/15th and 2/16th London Regiments were introduced for the first time to the line, while the enemy by every artifice at their command were putting impediments in the way. The reputation of the Labyrinth became still more unsavoury, no man knowing what new form the growing antagonism would assume.

The entrance of these new actors on the super-dramatic stage was unhappily marked by a hostile raid on our trenches at Sap 767. The battalion then in occupation lost six men killed and twenty wounded. To the troops under instruction, for the first time encountering a spirit of aggression, the experience might well have conveyed a feeling of fatal irresolution. Yet the young novitiate showed as bold a front as his case-hardened preceptor. Isolated parties of the fresh division, supported by Highland Territorials whom they were intended to relieve in the fullness of time, set the enemy so fiercely at defiance that their comrades, as yet unseasoned and lying in the deep caves of Aux Rietz, were carried away by their own fervent enthusiasm.

Among the many disturbing factors calculated to raise the apprehensions of untried soldiers were some that after a more proper appreciation weighed the balance in our favour. Such, for example, was the activity in the air, at first of dubious advantage, but on more mature judgment proved to be favourable to our wings. Such, also, was the constant roll of the artillery, until the ear, becoming more and more attuned to

IN THE WAKE OF THE PUSH

the varying volume of sound, hearkened at last to our own invincible guns.

The quick arrival of the London Division prompted innumerable inquiries in respect of our destination on relief. The multiplication of canards was uncountable. We were most partial to the rumour that we were going to a spot between Doullens and St. Pol, as G.H.Q. Reserve. Relief, however, was still denied us. The new division had to graduate through our hands.

All this time in the south events were marching. It was now the memorable first of July. At 2 p.m. signals reported that the first German trenches had been carried at Gommecourt. The message was very laconic, and nothing definite could be ascertained. The few rumours that were spread broadcast were mostly inflated and unlikely. It was not till 8 p.m. that another message, bearing the imprimatur of brigade signals, published the advance at La Boisselle and Hamel. The Great Push had commenced. All throughout the afternoon the guns roared without intermission. At 9.35 they became furious. I listened to them from the pretty road that skirts Etrun. They seemed to be very intense at Hebuterne. At 11 p.m. our artillery on the Vimy front began an aggressive diversion. The enemy, nervously expecting an assault, opened a rapid fire with all his arms. But there was no attack. We were merely trying his temper, wearing his nerves, and throwing his plans into confusion. For many days after this all ranks, expectant of sudden victory, had their hopes raised and as violently dashed down; for the news as officially circulated was alternately good and bad. Now it was the fall of Curlu. Now it was the capture of Fricourt. To balance these gains we were faced with the loss of Hamel and Gommecourt. We thought to judge all these things from a dispassionate point of view, for were we not going to be indulged with a long rest, far away from these terrible happenings?

But a strange feature of the present situation was that although we were presumably going out for a well-earned rest, drafts were still pouring in. Recently our numbers had been considerably increased. Our rifle strength, for a battalion in the line, was now

IN THE WAKE OF THE PUSH

abnormal. What was the meaning of all this careful replenishment? The more serious asked this question, but no answer was forthcoming—yet. One day, light was to break upon us, sharp and sudden.

The tone of the opposing enemy, though it could never have been called diffident, was now still more aggressive. His nerves were on edge. In this way was the keen fighting on the Somme reflected in the north. It was thought on good authority that the Prussian Guards had left our immediate front and had been succeeded by some cavalry. A change had certainly been effected. Many signs were noted confirmatory of this view. For the pulse of the enemy felt different. Apart from actual identification by raid, the critical eye could discover much from the merest change in the outward appearance of the trenches and the behaviour of the occupants. An unwary head might show a cap of different colour. In the present instance a difference was detected in the volume of fire, for fresh and nervous soldiers, it is well known, expend more rounds and are liable to more sudden panic than

IN THE WAKE OF THE PUSH

stolid veterans. Smoke now began to arise from the German support trenches, and this was a valuable clue, for it established beyond question the supposition that the opposing troops had come from a quiet sector, where fires had been permitted near the front line. In the case of such fires the principle of *laissez-faire* was often applied, both sides tacitly consenting to ignore such intimations of movement whereby men sought to make their rations more palatable or attempted to mitigate the evils of the cold weather. But no such humane truce ever alleviated the hardships of the Labyrinth. This new state of affairs soon resulted in increased casualties.

But if the Highland Division, worn out by unremitting toil, felt itself sorely buffeted by these blows, the 60th Division profited more and more by experience. The 2/15th and 2/16th Londons had had their baptism of fire, and the London Scottish now engaged our attention. Two companies were put into the Elbe Shelters, causing much congestion. The third company was relegated to the right supports, and the remaining company to the

IN THE WAKE OF THE PUSH

left. With such scanty accommodation at our disposal there was a great deal of unavoidable misery. One's heart bled for the men, shivering in the wet and having no means of neutralising their hardships. The two main communication trenches, Douai and Vase, were abominably wet. Indeed, from the supports upwards, Douai was almost impassable, and, being directly under the view of Vimy Ridge, was constantly exposed to mortar and musketry fire. The enemy took advantage of the bad weather to oppose all our endeavours to restore the integrity of the trenches. This was particularly the case on the north of Vimy Ridge. It will be remembered that a hurricane attack upon the Cheshires of such concentrated intensity that they were entirely withered away, had despoiled us of the northern spur of this ridge. Since that time the decision as to which party was to remain in possession was bitterly contested. At 1 a m. on July 9th, occurred one of those brief but violent exchanges of artillery which marked out Vimy as a place of evil notoriety. As dawn was coming over the shattered tree-tops of the ridge, the angry growl of the guns gradually died away.

In this mood of restrained gaiety and pardonable elation, in which I confess there was not seldom a tincture of disappointment at our inability to participate in the offensive, we looked forward to our rest. Our striking power, now impaired, would thereafter be irresistible. The moral fibre, at present debilitated by oppressive fatigues, would be reinforced. We hoped by a brief respite to reinvigorate the physical forces which months of sustained toil had threatened to subvert. From the remission of our labours we counted on emerging strengthened in body and confirmed in purpose.

On July 14th the march of light hearts and leaden feet began. We quitted Ecoivres at 9 o'clock in the morning, shaping our course towards St. Pol. And our eyes, which for many months had never gazed upon an intact roof, or a field that was not cursed with shells and sanctified with crosses, or a tree that was not blasted and decaying, now witnessed villages unsullied by war, rich pastures and abundant crops, and the broad leafy

IN THE WAKE OF THE PUSH

avenues of Capelle, Aubigny, and Savy. Mulvey had gone ahead with the billeting party; and speculation was rife as to the nature of our prospective billets. When at length we diverged from the national road and struck out for Marquay the pleasant transition almost unsettled our jaded minds. At that moment we gave ourselves up to anticipated joys, ejecting all morbid recollections and postponing the thought of harsh times to come. Plans were being laid already for concerts and carousals. The sports committee proposed football matches. Pitches were recommended for the sports which might profitably yield both amusement and exercise. We were indeed basking in the sunshine of fair hopes.

But now all our hopes and new-born joys were dashed down as violently as they had been raised; for a courier had come with strange tidings. The peaceful seclusion of Marquay was to be ours not even for a night. We were to be hurried off to an unknown destination. Whither, no one knew. All that was vouchsafed us was that motor-lorries were to remove the brigade that very night.

IN THE WAKE OF THE PUSH

Officers' kits were now reduced to the required minimum. Surplus kit was stacked and laid aside. G.S. wagons were laden and limbers filled up to the limit of their establishment. At 9.40 lorries arrived for the transport of the whole battalion, and by midnight a three-mile length of lorries sped southwards with headlights blazing. All along the route, till it was held up at the railway crossing at Frévent, the wagon convoy presented a sight that must live for ever, even in the most unretentive mind. It was a very clear night. Sometimes a peak of colour on the horizon told where the embattled troops were striving for the mastery. In the morning we reached Halloy; and two days later made the village of Berneuil.

IX HIGH WOOD

WE were now no longer operating as part of the Third Army, but were to be counted as effectives of the Fifth Army Reserve. And the significance of this was not wholly lost upon us, for hereafter it was but a short step into the Fourth Army engaged in the Somme offensive. There could be no doubt now about the issue. All dreams of rest vanished into thin air. Very soon we knew that we would be locked in a life-and-death struggle with the enemy. But where . . . ? Reason pointed to Pozières; rumour, with more irresolute finger, to Gommecourt. News was constantly arriving from the front. The last definite report had been received at Halloy, when it was made known that the envelopment of Pozières was in progress, and that heavy fighting was expected in that quarter. In the meantime, preparations closely affecting ourselves began to be made

HIGH WOOD

for the coming blow. As yet, however, no information of an official warranty leaked out concerning our movements. But only one conclusion could be drawn from the thorough examination of equipment and the issue of trench maps delineating the battle-front of the Somme. As far, too, as was compatible with discipline and efficiency, the men were given release from all trying fatigues, and a short route march to Gorges, interrupted as it was by heavy rains, was deemed sufficient to uphold the standard of both these qualities. The weather, which had been dull and cloudy, now assumed a more promising aspect. And the spirit of the troops rose in proportion, till on all sides were heard expressions of the utmost enthusiasm. The acme of sanguine hopes was reached at Brigade Head-quarters, which may have been due to the comfort and serenity of their surroundings.

Being continually in a state of readiness, we were not unprepared for sudden movement orders. The first intimation was received at 8 o'clock on the 19th, the transport being ordered to Flesselles without

HIGH WOOD

delay. Expectant, we lay down to a fitful rest. At 2 a.m. an orderly knocked at my door and said that the whole battalion was aroused and likely to move within an hour. Then the two old women with whom I happened to be billeted arose and prepared a meal of coffee and eggs, and insisted on filling my water-bottle with cider. Before light had set in the brigade was on the march, shaping its course through Fienvillers, beyond which, sleeping by the roadside and shivering in the early mists, we passed the 4th Seaforths. Meanwhile the transport had been redirected from Flesselles to Méricourt. At 7.30 a.m. we entrained at Candas, where other troops, battle-stained and cheerful, laughed at us through the mud and filth which days of incessant fighting had imprinted on their faces. It was the first visible sign of the great offensive. The troop-train crawled slowly away, past Montrelet and St. Ouen, following the valley of the Nièvre, where all that is most beautiful in nature seemed to be crystallised in the village of Fieffes. Weeds were growing up between the metals and untrimmed bushes overhung the embankments. In the minds of some all the quietude of the valley inspired a false confidence, and, to add to the illusion, the optimistic chatterers maintained that we were now pursuing a course directly opposite to that which ought to take us to the front. They did not know, however, that this branch line united with the main railroad from Abbeville to Albert. And the crossing of the viaduct over the Somme marshes soon brought us to the trunk line leading to the heart of the hostilities.

To our disappointment the train passed through the fine station of Amiens without stopping, the market gardens slipped by, the little vignettes of Senegalese troops became a blur in the memory, Corbie of old acquaintance faded from our view, and at 2 o'clock we steamed into railhead, Méricourt-Ribemont. Those of us who had known Méricourt of old (for we had detrained here in July 1915) were amazed at the change. Then, it had been a little sleepy station with a few sidings and a tent or two for the accommodation of prospective permissionnaires. Now it was the busy centre of all the traffic

HIGH WOOD

in men and material feeding the firing line in the sector of Albert. Immense stores of provisions and piles of ammunition lay stacked ready for transport. German prisoners, mostly unshaven, were engaged in road-mending, or were lazily watching the new troops.

Under a blazing sun we marched out of the station. Buire-sur-Ancre showed unmistakable signs of activity. Tired men were dragging themselves along the hot, dusty road, traces of recent fighting plain upon their faces. A few attempted to smile. Sweat ran down and grooved the dirt on their foreheads and cheeks. Many lacked full equipment. Regiments came out under the command of subalterns, careworn and ageing. Limbers and wagons were rushing up towards the line with food for the men or ammunition for the guns. In happy contrast to the stricken remnants returning from battle were the kilted troops now marching on Dernancourt. Meanwhile the 154th Brigade went to Méaulte, two kilometres farther on. The 152nd Brigade had not arrived, but was expected at any moment. Close billets

HIGH WOOD

alone were available in Dernancourt, where the town-major had a particularly trying experience in accommodating battalion after battalion in a very restricted area. Confusion at such a time and place, however, was unavoidable.

Now part of the Fourth, or combatant, Army, we began to get first-hand news of its performances. Tales of success were inspiring everybody to deal a more final blow than had yet been delivered. As yet, of course, it was purely prospective courage. The testing time was to come. Particularly inspiring was the news that the 2nd Gordons had attacked that morning with signal success. The spirit of emulation was aroused. At 2 p.m. on the 20th movement orders arrived, and with them instructions to reconnoitre the position identified by the map references S 14a to S 15d, which comprised the old German second line between the two Bazentins. We held, however, a considerable extent of ground beyond this, as far as the edge of High Wood. The divisional frontage was amazingly small, being no more than a slight extension on either side of the

HIGH WOOD

Bois des Foureaux. My division relieved the 33rd and at the end of the day was disposed as follows:

The 154th Brigade occupied the line, with the 153rd Brigade in support and the 152nd Brigade in reserve. The 154th Brigade had three battalions in the trench fringing High Wood and one battalion fully a thousand yards behind in local support at the Crucifix. The supporting brigade lay in the deep folds of the ground between Caterpillar and Mametz woods. And the brigade in reserve was in comfortable bivouac near Fricourt and Bécordel. We were flanked on the left by the 19th Division and on the right by the 5th Division.

The immensity of the push was now apparent to us, and our eyes opened in astonishment at the awful havoc of the guns. We, who had seen over twelve months' service, astonished! A giant of steel seemed to have ridden over the proud German defences. Villages were wiped completely out of existence; woods were laid waste. Saddest sight of all, there was not a blade of green grass visible. A tumbled heap of rubble marked the spot where the church of Fricourt once stood. Its very bricks were powdered to dust. A few gable ends still stood in Mametz. These were being gradually demolished by enemy fire. Trenches were everywhere blown out of recognition. Disrupted sand-bags littered the broken earth. In every direction disused gunpits with piles of empty shell-cases showed how the artillery had advanced. A poignant reminder that victory is not purchased without cost lay in the mounds of newly delved earth where blue flags were fluttering over the dead.

The transport lay in bivouac in what had been No Man's Land between Bécourt and Fricourt Village. From this point of vantage much of the terrible drama was visible. Not an inch of ground but was covered by war material and troops resting. Mametz Road presented an unparalleled scene of activity. Never for an instant was it idle. There were up roads and down roads everywhere. Ammunition, food, guns, went up the one in constant streams; wounded and fatigued men, empty ammunition and ration limbers, came rolling back on the other. Whenever any thoroughfare showed signs of disrepair, either by shell-fire or natural consumption, gangs of men from labour battalions set to work, metalling and restoring. These men were nearly all over age. They had none of the hot glory of conflict. To them fell no soul-stirring battle honours. Yet who but must admire the spirit that sent these gallant veterans into the zone of shell-fire.

The view of the fighting from the actual front was of necessity local. But here a much broader outlook was possible. The immense superiority of the guns in the first place struck the observer. And then, one could not fail to be impressed with our mastery of the air.

The guns were everywhere, *ubique*. The two Bazentins were nests of field guns. Round Mametz Wood and in the adjacent valley howitzer batteries showed the ugly snouts of their pieces from every conceivable quarter. They were literally wheel to wheel. Recalling those dark days of 1915, when we implored the gunners for support and implored in vain, now it made one's heart

HIGH WOOD

rejoice to see those inexhaustible stacks of shells and to hear the guns roaring without intermission. North-west of Fricourt a battery of Australian 9·2's lay in position. Hard by were ten French guns of 120 mm. calibre. They looked deadly precise weapons, nosing the air as if scenting an unseen prey.

How terribly the enemy had been blinded became daily more obvious. The hum of aircraft rung in the ears continually. All day long the droning battleplane wheeled over the scene of carnage. Reconnoitring planes flew backwards and forwards with information of enemy masses, train movements, and gun positions. The more humble contact aeroplanes hung a few hundred feet over the advancing troops and reported progress to the artillery. They flew unperturbed through the avalanche of our own shells. Whenever an objective was attained by the infantry, coloured flares ascended, and the contact aeroplane immediately conveyed the intelligence to the gunners, who lengthened their range and prepared the ground for further advance.

THE SPECTRAL SKELETON OF FRI-
COURT CHÂTEAU, NOW A HEAP OF
POWDERED BRICKS

HIGH WOOD

But not only in aeroplanes were we seemingly supreme. Observational work by aircraft was necessarily hasty and brief. It was the captive balloon that supplied the more detailed and continuous information. These balloons were connected to earth by telephone. On the Somme front, when the light was good, I have counted as many as twenty-five swinging lazily in the breeze. Indeed, the increasing salient of our battle front, as we bit deeper and deeper into the German defences, could be gauged by the wide crescent of these aerial outposts.

I have said that the transport was bivouacked in the vicinity of Fricourt. With the transport remained a certain proportion of commissioned and non-commissioned officers. They were held here as reinforcements to replace almost unavoidable casualties. Into action the battalion could take but twenty officers. From the impedimenta of captured trenches the remainder made temporary shelters until such time as they were called upon to fill gaps in their respective ranks. All the "standbacks" awaited such a summons from this

HIGH WOOD

historic spot. And surely never did history show itself so poignant as here. It was the scene of more Homeric encounters than had ever been witnessed before in the world. The eye, travelling over the awful waste, saw nothing but the earth churned out of all recognition. On the right, the Tambour and the Bois Français seemed to have been shattered by a cataclysmic upheaval. On the left, La Boisselle and Fricourt were both shivered into such a ghastly state of annihilation that their fragmentary remains could scarcely be recognised.

Not only above, but underneath, had this amazing tornado passed. Human moles had burrowed with an uncanny sense of direction right underneath those ingeniously contrived subterranean passages. They had prepared, with an immense amount of patience, self-sacrifice, and danger, daring not only detection by the enemy, but also the far more insidious peril of poison gas, mines beside which those of the Labyrinth shrunk into pettiness. And then in a moment, by the mere pressure of an electric button, in a mighty convulsion they had overwhelmed

HIGH WOOD

all those galleries and caverns where the enemy was cowering under the avalanche of our shells. Yet some parts of this desolated region awoke the feeling of gentle reminiscence instead of oppressing the mind with the sense of awful tragedy. Twelve months previously our acquaintance with these places sympathetically attracted us to them. We had given them Highland names, stamping them for all time with the seal of Celticism. Once more I had the opportunity of wandering over our old haunts. In Bécourt Wood *Mulviross Villa* still stood intact, howbeit a little departed from its pristine splendour.

Hitherto Mametz Valley, since its capture from the enemy, had suffered but little from hostile shelling; but now the heavies were being brought up and the old positions ranged to a nicety. The valley soon became one of the hottest parts of the front. The Germans poured a prodigal amount of ammunition into it. And it was easy to observe how effective such a mass of fire could be when this was the only avenue by which rations could be brought up to the infantry or

HIGH WOOD

ammunition to the guns. It was a ceaseless menace, too, to the approach of reinforcements, and reliefs were apt to suffer greatly, if caught here by a chance bombardment—a chance bombardment, because the enemy could no longer see the results of his fire. He dared not risk his observation balloons. In this veritable valley of death, the 153rd Brigade hung on to their precarious recesses among the tangles of roots. Rarely were nerves tested in this fashion before. One had to submit patiently to the terrible punishment, knowing that soon would come the time for cold steel and the relentless driving power of vengeance.

On the 21st tear-shells began to fall. Gas-shells also were not uncommon. The detonation of these gas-shells was almost unheard. These tear- and gas-shell bombardments continued at intervals, but night was the time when the enemy was most disposed to employ such agents.

On the 22nd and the 23rd, our artillery seemed to be exerting itself up to the utmost. There was no pause to the breathless roulade. Sometimes the fire slackened, but never for

HIGH WOOD

an instant ceased. On the 23rd the guns were particularly violent, in preparation for the assault that was to make the Australians masters of Pozières. On this day, too, the 154th Brigade were reported to have made an attack on the German positions at High Wood, passing through such a devastating curtain fire that their attacks were broken down. The battalions engaged were the 4th Gordons and the 9th Royal Scots, the " Dandy Ninth," the supporting regiments in Mametz meanwhile standing to. The assault was vain, and the division crouched for the next spring.

It was my good fortune to be for a time among the reinforcement reserves. So far the battalion was singularly free from heavy casualties, and for a time there was no call made upon our resources. Though under occasional shell-fire we formed a very happy and contented company. Some of the scenes indeed are unforgettable. Friendships were cemented here as never before. A solemn impressiveness gripped all hearts in those fateful hours. On the Sunday, a church service, conducted by Padre Watson, strove

HIGH WOOD

to regenerate the minds that by reason of familiarity with death were too liable to be drowsed by the opiate of religious indifference. The gathering was small and the address short, for military needs dictated that men should not be assembled in large numbers. By those ever-famous craters, singing as of old in the conventicles of Galloway, softly poured the strains in contrast to the deep booming of the guns.

> " Jesu, lover of my soul,
> Let me to Thy bosom fly."

During the night 26/27th the artillery battle continued with unrelenting severity. For hours an unbroken sequence of sound drummed along the fighting front, and the ground shook as if ague-stricken. The focus of intensity varied each hour from flank to flank. Sometimes, as at early dawn, the scene of grimmest endeavour was on our immediate front. High Wood stank with gas, which penetrated to our supporting positions at the Bazentins, and even inflicted casualties on the troops occupying Caterpillar and Mametz Woods.

At 5 a.m., the weather being dull but pro-

HIGH WOOD

mising and visibility good, a hurricane fire was opened on Martinpuich and Delville. On the previous night the 5th Division were reported to be massing for an attack on Delville Wood. Subsequent reports, indicating the capture of that ghastly arena of bloodshed, would seem to convey that the attack materialised. The Germans, though sorely harassed by our galling fire, directed not only against their trenches and batteries, but also against their rest-billets and communications, did not submit tamely to punishment. Notwithstanding the random nature of their retaliation, they were able to cause us considerable discomfort. Blinded as they were, yet their shooting could not be called wild. And they took the advantage of favourable atmospheric conditions, particularly in gas attacks, to attain the maximum effect. Their range of shelling alternated from Mametz to Fricourt. Again our air supremacy, hitherto unchallenged, was now hotly contested. Some of the finest German wings were brought up to restore the balance. But it was almost impossible to make leeway, and on few occasions only were German airmen able to evade our patrols and make a hasty reconnaissance of our foremost and rear positions. At 5 p.m. three enemy aircraft ventured across for a period sufficiently prolonged to enable them to locate precisely where our rest-camps and our bivouacs were situated, and we waited for the artillery storm to break upon us. An immense explosion in the direction of Montauban, which piled columns of smoke high into the air, for the moment distracted our attention from the engagements among the clouds.

On the 28th, the 153rd Brigade relieved the 154th Brigade in the line. It was known that an attack on High Wood was impending. The favourable opportunity was awaited with ill-concealed impatience. The exploitation of a successful push demands the most exacting preparation, the essential requirement being a precise co-operation between infantry and artillery; otherwise our brave battalions become, to use an expressive German phrase, " Kanonenfutter." Very detailed information, secured by the resourcefulness of patrols, the intelligent

HIGH WOOD

interrogation of prisoners, and the daring reconnaissances of aeroplanes, are the only means whereby suitability of target can be guaranteed to the guns. Events proved that in the subsequent assaults on High Wood too little was known regarding its state of defence. For however intense the shelling, it was not yet intense enough to break down the resistance of the defending garrison. Although it was now common knowledge that the 51st Division would launch an offensive in conjunction with the 19th Division on the left and the 5th Division on the right, the actual zero-time was not positively fixed; or, if it was, secrecy was well maintained. It was stated that fifty deserters to the 5th Division reported preparations for a German counter-attack on their lost positions before Longueval. This attack materialised, but failed to achieve success.

On the 29th more and more fire was concentrated on the enemy. Tons of metal were hurled into High Wood and the hurriedly designed switch-line running from it to Flers. Its trees were uprooted and its timbers twisted and split and slivered. But a wood

HIGH WOOD

must be utterly devastated if an attack upon it is to make any progress. Merely swept down, it becomes a man-trap. Here the Germans, wonderfully tenacious of ground, wired the fallen branches, made obstacles of tree trunks, and established well posted machine guns in the corner of the wood. It was such a formidable objective that faced the brigade on the 30th, when the final orders were issued. During the afternoon an intensive bombardment prepared the way for the assaulting units. At times it increased to a drum-fire. The preliminary bombardment began at 4.45 and continued till 6.15. The brigade took up position as follows: The 7th Black Watch were opposite High Wood. On their right extended the 6th Black Watch. Still farther to the right lay the 5th Gordons. The 7th Gordons were in support near the Crucifix. At Mametz Wood the 152nd Brigade lay in readiness for any emergency as divisional supports. The 154th Brigade were withheld as divisional reserve at Bécordel. The 19th Division, it will be remembered, were co-operating on our left and the 5th Division on our right.

HIGH WOOD

The hour of zero was **6.15**. At that moment the guns lifted, and the assaulting waves leapt over the parapet. They were instantly met by a well-sustained fire from trenches that seemed to be amply manned and plentifully munitioned. From the very beginning the attack was doomed to frustration. By those awful sheets of cross-fire men were mown down in swathes. The 7th Black Watch, embarrassed by the treacherous pitfalls and blocked by a thick *réseau* of barbed wire, were shot down in great numbers. By **7.30** p.m. the situation was dangerous. Everywhere the assault had broken down. A *précis* of the reports received an hour after the initiation of the attack established the fact that the 7th Black Watch had sustained severe losses. Among the officers Captains Boase and Gillespie were known to be dead. To balance this loss a slight forward thrust had been made, but the enemy's trenches were nowhere penetrated. Digging operations had to be resorted to. The other two battalions, similarly affected and with proportionate losses, were forced to earth. They

HIGH WOOD

could neither advance nor withdraw, and their casualties were mounting up at an alarming rate. Urgent appeals were therefore made to the 7th Gordons for assistance. Platoon by platoon these reinforced the firing line till all but three were absorbed. They had to pass through terrific bursts of curtain fire, but by a singular good fortune escaped without heavy losses. At 9.45 the attack on the left was resumed, and both artilleries blazed into a new *accès* of fury. The divisions on either flank had achieved moderate successes. All night long the enemy poured destructive fire on our positions.

It was deemed advisable that the 7th Black Watch should be replaced by the 7th Gordons. Instructions, therefore, were issued to that effect, and the relief was completed by 4 p.m. on the 31st without incident. A clear review of the situation now shed interesting light on the murderous fighting that marked this disputed wood as one of the grimmest charnel houses on the Somme. The wood became each day a more and more sombre *morgue*. All living things within it seemed to be fated to extinction. Yet at no time could the shelling of our trenches be characterised as severe. The enemy was conspicuously nervous. He opened barrages for no apparent reason, and flung away an incalculable amount of ammunition which spent itself to no advantage in the hollow ground behind High Wood. On our left the advanced trenches of the enemy were clearly within view. On our right the flaming embers of Longueval were spurting high in horrid red spears. In all this upheaved area the earth was spouting in huge black cataracts, and the air was charged with dense clouds of smoke. In some places cones of fire rained down from heaven and great white banks of cumulus rose up and slowly dissipated.

The switch-line of the enemy and his lateral retrenchments for converging fire were admirably sited to frustrate any further offensive. Until the preparation, therefore, could be made overwhelming, no offensive was planned for the immediate future. Nor did it seem, after the lapse of a few days, that the Germans would initiate a counter-blow. Inaction, however, can never be laid to their

HIGH WOOD

charge. Each day saw their defences, so seriously threatened, grow more formidable. Their pioneers were tireless. Their " Betontruppen," specialists in the erection of concrete machine-gun emplacements, and their " Hollenbaukommandos " for the construction of dug-outs, were organising a newly formed system of trenches on a scale of great magnitude, and with the invaluable accessories of intermediate strong points. Trenches, wired and traversed, emerged in a single night. The favourable features of the ground were everywhere transformed into miniature fortresses of amazing strength, from whose loop-holed bastions machine-guns in countless numbers pushed their deadly muzzles.

The brigade, exhausted by their toils, stifled by the heat and dust, and almost unmanned by the shambles around them, on the first day of August went into bivouac at Buire as divisional reserve. The 152nd Brigade relieved us, my unit handing over to the 6th Gordons.

X   A CITY IN CELLARS

For many days no recollection of these horrors was permitted to diminish the enthusiasm of the division. Concerts were held nightly. On the bare slopes near Méaulte the infantry, worn out by their recent trials, engaged themselves in innocent relaxation. "The Balmorals," the theatre party of the division, addressed themselves to their congenial offices with a diligence no less justified of the times than it was deserving of support. Blood had freely flown, and would flow again as freely. In the meantime no dejection of spirits must be allowed to usurp the place of contentment and good cheer. The guns were still ranged solidly against the enemy and pulverising his trenches. His own artillery, admittedly well handled, was redoubling its opposition. More and more troops, eager to win renown and excited by unwonted activity, were pouring up towards the line. Observation balloons, marshalled in ever-increasing numbers, were night and day foiling the secret movements of the enemy. Defeated and despairing, the Germans, stung to a paroxysm of frenzy, were hurling themselves on their lost positions. Forfeiture of ground, privations unproclaimed, renunciation of hope, submission and subjugation—all these things they had been taught to abhor. And now, as we forced them to accept adversity, they resisted with fierce courage.

For the present we were not to be re-engaged upon the Somme, but, transported to Long Pré, were moved into quarters at Citernes. It was not thought improbable that the division would be recalled to scenes exceeding even the horrors of High Wood. But the days passed quietly, until on August 11th we entrained at Long Pré and moved to the north. In the early afternoon we passed through Abbeville. The tented dunes of Étaples swarmed with reinforcements. As darkness descended we entered the region of the flats of Flanders. The coast line receded. Boulogne and Calais

ST. OMER

A CITY IN CELLARS

were left far behind. St. Omer and Hazebrouck were before us. Soon these, too, were swallowed up in the night. At 11 p.m. we detrained at Thiennes and marched away. As dawn was breaking officers and men threw themselves down to snatch a little sleep in billets already provided at Racquinghem.

Although we felt ourselves a little disappointed with our renewed acquaintance with the Flemish fogs, *pavés*, and *polders*, we gradually adapted ourselves to the changed conditions. A year had made a vast difference in our powers of appreciation. Casting back to those grim days of Festubert, there stood out in bold relief pools rotting with dead, trenches constructionally weak, and an enemy gunnery the mastery of which was denied to us for many a long day to come. But the passing of twelve months had shown us, week by week, such striking improvements that there was now no limit to our confidence. All these things reacted favourably on our outlook. Our fickle minds recalled only the monotony of the rolling Picard uplands. They were now touched by the vision of a new beauty.

A CITY IN CELLARS

Billeting in Racquinghem was exceptionally good. The farms were clean and sweet. There was no uncomfortable overcrowding. Most of the officers slept in the empty rooms of a deserted château. The field officers were housed with the *curé*. A charming little *couturière* in the village offered me the use of a room which she was at some pains to make comfortable. Her father, who was the village wheelwright, never tired of telling me about the dark days of '70–'71. I warmed to Racquinghem.

For four days the battalion enjoyed immunity from the strain of exacting work. The usual parades were held to preserve discipline and efficiency. These parades took place as a rule on the summit of some rising ground hard by, clothed in an exotic garb of blazing purple heather. After the routine of daily parades and inspections it was customary for a few of us to ride or cycle into St. Omer, about eleven kilometres distant. St. Omer was the point of convergence for the military on the northern front, just as Bethune was for the La Bassée sector, St. Pol for the Vimy Ridge, Doullens

A CITY IN CELLARS

for Hébuterne, and Amiens for the Somme. It was the half-way house to Calais. The amenities of St. Omer could not be excelled in another town of equal size. Its parks, even in war-time, were beautifully laid out and kept in irreproachable condition. The *beau-monde* of St. Omer loved to dawdle in the gardens during these fine summer evenings, speculating on the *étalage* of officers, drawn by the enchantments of a beautiful and refreshing retreat, who seemed in their turn to attract, by the mere glitter of orders or the cut of a becoming tunic, the coquettish multitude. Many a man in his proud mail of military punctilio here capitulated to some alluring and *dégagée* goddess. An attractive war-time gaiety pervaded the whole town. Troops of various nationalities and regiments strolled about the boulevards or sat sipping coffee in the restaurants. Blue and khaki uniforms intermixed in the streets everywhere. Cadets wearing green bands were to be encountered at every corner. Flying Corps officers seemed to monopolise the club in the Grand Place. About the easy manners of the *boulevardier* there was

A CITY IN CELLARS

an inexplicable charm, which, try as we might, we could never hope to imitate.

For four clear days we were left to our own devices at Racquinghem. But at length movement orders arrived, sooner than we expected, and at 4 a.m. on the 16th the transport rattled out noisily on the cobbled road. The start of the infantry was delayed for a few hours. Finally, in consort with the 5th Gordons we entrained at Ebblinghem.

The battalion went into billets that night at Armentières. It had detrained at Steenwerck and marched by a circuitous route. When the history of this front comes to be written to tell posterity how the Armentiérois, only two miles from the line, refused to abandon their broken houses, it must surely prove one of the most sublime records of fortitude. Dispossessed of their effects by shell-fire, unnerved by constant bombardments, exposed every moment of their lives to the danger of mutilation or death, hundreds elected to remain, prosecuting their business or attending to their family needs. The Rue de Dunkerque invariably presented a scene of the utmost activity, women

A CITY IN CELLARS

bustling about in small shops and disposing of their wares at advantageous prices. It was inevitable in the circumtances that these prices should be enormously enhanced, and the wonder is that they were not altogether prohibitive. Some of the shops were pathetic. Near the junction of the Rue Nationale and the Rue de Dunkerque the "Lady from Lille," a fugitive from the fury of the invader, spread on her counters the latest English journals and periodicals.

Some streets escaped the horrors of gradual demolition by gunfire, as if the wings of a guardian angel were beating over them. It was only a reprieve. Sooner or later the whistling shells found out the refuges. Other streets, ravaged and despoiled, seemed to have been marked out for the special visitation of evil.

The churches were everywhere reduced and desecrated. Of the Church of Notre Dame the fine façade was swept away. On one occasion, while flying over the town, I watched the sun flame up from the Church of St. Roch, a mere illusion of splendour, for this church was an abomination of ruin.

A CITY IN CELLARS

The people of Armentières retired to their cellars when the city was experiencing the savagery of the Germans; but at other times they walked abroad with an expression of the greatest aplomb. For many months, Lucienne, in her little tea-shop in the Place de la République, regaled the thirsty wayfarer. At the Hôtel du Bœuf, near the Mairie, an excellent dinner was invariably served. Indeed, we messed here on the first night of our arrival in order to fête one who, in virtue of his age and splendid service, although he would have been the last man to admit it himself, had been given the position of Town Major of Heilly-Ribemont. The indifference of the waitresses to the imminence of a sudden and dreadful death was truly remarkable. The day before our arrival, a girl, the most beautiful in Armentières, was blown to pieces in her cellar by a shell which tore through the flimsy walls and exploded in the very place where she was taking protection.

But where we expected to find dejection and low spirits, we found instead vivacity and mirth. Order and high courage pre-

A CITY IN CELLARS

vailed over confusion and despondency. Labour in the city stopped with automatic regularity when the cannonade became hot, but when quiet again supervened it was resumed without any appearance of fluster. The Tissage near the Quai de la Dérivation lay with its looms idle and rusting, but the caretaker and his entire family still remained courageously at their posts. From the chimneys of the large and important factories near the Pont de Nieppe smoke still issued; work was not yet interdicted; barges came down the Lys, made fast by the walls, and departed with their quondam freights. The shelling of Armentières did not serve to interrupt the work or agitate the workers, who at the close of day might have been seen in chattering groups returning to their cellar homes. Such were the people—patient in adversity, pertinacious in defence, proud to resist the invader, jealous in the guardianship of their privileges and liberties—against whom the Germans vainly matched their arms.

With each successive victory on the Somme the whole Western front lost the extreme rigidity that had characterised it in times of comparative quiet. The constant focussing of troops in the south meant a very fluid state of affairs elsewhere. There was an unprecedented interchange of divisions. As each division came out of the conflict, enfeebled by its experiences and wanting the dynamic force necessary for a further assault, it was sent to a sector where the pressure was not so severe. The division relieved by the Highlanders, energised by the first flush of tourney, gravitated as a matter of course to the Mecca of all keen soldiers, the Somme. This state of flux, however, was common to both friend and foe. The enemy also found it necessary to make his line as elastic as possible. Until recently the XIXth German Army Corps held the Armentières front. It was relieved by the VIth Reserve Army Corps, withdrawn from the Somme. Reading from north to south the order of battle about this time seems to have been the 22nd Infantry Regiment, the 10th Reserve Infantry Regiment, and the 156th Infantry Regiment. Dealing in particular with our own brigade front, the enemy until quite a

A CITY IN CELLARS

recent date held the line as follows: The 179th Regiment was responsible for the safety of the front from the River Lys to 4 Hallots Farm, and the 133rd Regiment extended that responsibility as far as Brune Fine. These were relieved respectively by the 22nd Regiment and the 11th Reserve Regiment, both belonging to the 11th Reserve Division.

Till the 22nd we remained in Armentières, fast by a factory, enjoying thoroughly the bliss of idleness and a contented lazy stupor of mind. Every officer had paid a visit to the trenches in order to study their peculiarities, and come back enthusiastic in their praise. They found them hushed and peaceful. Sometimes the hush was broken when the Germans flung minenwerfer into the Orchard, or among the tumbled stones of Hobbs' Farm.

The Germans directed most of their fire on that rectangular hedge-bordered block, known as the Orchard. But the devastating torpedoes plunged uselessly into the shrubs, tearing great holes but causing little material damage.

A CITY IN CELLARS

On August 24th hot and close weather gave place to some smart showers. The wind blew from the south-west in an unfavourable direction for enemy gas. A few minenwerfer in the gap separating us from the 7th Argyll and Sutherlands failed to achieve any success. The random torpedoes ceased and the forenoon passed in a phenomenal calm. The sun came out and shone on the red roofs of Houplines. It was now fine weather, and both sides were enjoying an unofficial armistice. Head-quarters sat under a willow tree in the open, busily preparing defence schemes. The men were cheerfully executing their appointed tasks without suffering the slightest interruption. But this display of inertness was quite unnatural. At 5 o'clock we resumed activity with our trench mortars, provoking a prompt retaliation which came from Les 4 Hallots, and, striking the Orchard diagonally, shattered still more the fruitless trees. This oblique fire was noticeably of very long range, the extreme estimate being about one thousand yards. The practice of engaging the Orchard as a target for the trench mortars was quickly discontinued when our artillery, awaiting the moment of attack, opened with sudden and fierce violence. Next day the enemy found it necessary to alter his programme. The afternoon "strafe" became a morning salutation, and ere long he was forced to dispose his mortars where our artillery had no registered target.

When we were in immediate support to the line we remained in Houplines. At other times we retired to Armentières and Bailleul. On the 29th we were enjoying a temporary relaxation at Houplines, in a château whose sole link with past luxury was a broken-down Bord. A raid had been arranged for this night. Gas was to be liberated so as to paralyse opposition; but bad weather intervened, and the wind veered round till it was no longer from a favourable quarter. The cancellation of the raid was therefore intimated, although hopes were ardently expressed that the postponement would not be long enough to suffer a diminution of enthusiasm. On the succeeding day the barometer fell, heavy rains ensuing, with gusty squalls of wind. Towards nightfall

A CITY IN CELLARS

the high wind moderated, and with this welcome abatement came also a change in direction. It was decided therefore to put into instant execution the raiding scheme formulated by the 6th Black Watch, then in the line. A message was received in code that the hour of zero would be half-past one. I crept into my valise, with implicit instructions to be awakened at 1.15.

Before the raiders were in their appointed places it was discovered, or suspected, by the troops in the line that a hostile relief was in progress. Rarely does such a unique opportunity present itself. Two minutes before zero, bursts of machine-gun fire began, principally to deaden the peculiar hissing sound made by the emission of gas. Precisely at half-past one the first jet of gas was released. Three more followed in quick succession. There was no hostile fire, but within three minutes a great shouting and sudden confusion were audible in the German lines. An intensive bombardment of the wire by our artillery lifted and became a protective barrage, falling upon the enemy's support trenches. And at this moment the

A CITY IN CELLARS

raiders left the trenches. About 2.45 suspicions were aroused that the raiding party was engaged too long in its perilous enterprise. It now appeared that a sequence of unfortunate accidents prevented what would otherwise have proved a very successful minor action. At the very outset a light shell, bursting in their ranks, made seven of the raiders casualties. At 2.45 an officer stumbled in, all perspiration. He had been superintending the smoke-bombs, and could only tell us that the gas went over well at an angle. Two asteroids bursting into showers of gold and silver were to have intimated to the artillery that all was over. In vain we watched for these rockets, until the artillery, suspecting that something was wrong, gradually decreased their fire. When I returned to my interrupted sleep the guns were still booming in a desultory fashion.

Morning dawned. An air of cheerful quiet pervaded the ruins of Houplines. Some bathers were plunging with delightful abandon in the muddy Lys, where a small backwater ran forbiddingly round the Château Rose. Some one was strumming a music-hall ditty on the old Bord. Batmen were busily frying bacon and polishing Sam Brownes alternately. And on retrospect it crept into my head that Death, after all, is nothing. It is an incident of war. It is round and about us wherever we go—under our feet, in the air above, before and behind us. A quiet dawn! ... and on the stretchers in the dressing station are gathered the bleeding remains of heroes who will raid no more.

The Germans often attempted to take sleeping troops by surprise. Without the slightest warning they were accustomed to pour a violent fire on all places where they thought our soldiers might be resting or in reserve. Civilians frequently suffered in these periodical outbursts. But from a military point of view the expense of powder and shot was not commensurate with the results attained. The situation, generally considered, continued to be eminently satisfactory. But for the enemy, who found his mortars or his guns engaged every time that they opened, the prospect was unpleasant. All along the Armentières front the offensive

A CITY IN CELLARS

spirit was being steadily fostered in order that there would be no opportunity for the enemy to withdraw troops to a sector open to a threat. Nearly every night saw his trenches raided at one point or another. Whenever the wind was favourable, gas was liberated against him. The guns were constantly seeking out some new target. Now it would be Les 4 Hallots, now it would be Perenchies. Or the fortified outskirts of Lille would suffer at our hands. And when we heard the long-range shells whining over to Lille, we knew instinctively that retaliation would bring forth repentance in Armentières.

Bailleul was one of those places eminently suited to recruit our flagging energies. The air was invigorating, for the town rose substantially higher than the surrounding country. It was very rarely shelled, and then only by long-range guns. When we repaired hither the thunder of the guns was heard to be sensibly diminished. The shops were plentiful and abundantly stocked. There was at least one good hotel, and in the Rue d'Occident a little alley, the residence of

A CITY IN CELLARS

"Tina," suddenly sprang into fame. Tina, it was commonly reported, sold the best beer in France, and indeed she attracted to her parlour a *clientèle* as extensive as it was respectful. For Tina brooked no unseemly disorders to bring her house into disrepute. She was both young and charming, spoke English with a command of idiom that took the listener by surprise, was dignified in her carriage and complaisant in her demeanour.

To this town, whose sole industrial support was lace-making, the battalion marched on September 13th, taking over comfortable bivouacs. In the meantime, however, the constant harassing of the enemy was accentuated by a double raid undertaken with much energy and spirit by the 7th Gordons and the 7th Black Watch.

The day selected for this enterprise, September 14th, was singularly unpropitious. The weather, though improving, was still cold and wet. But a second disappointment could not be allowed to cool the ardour of the men who had volunteered for an office so fraught with danger. Nothing was wanting from the preparations to ensure a com-

A CITY IN CELLARS

plete success. The men were all filled with a quiet confidence in their leaders.

At length all was ready and the men in their places, the Gordons on the left and the Black Watch on the right. The Engineers were rapidly supervising the emplacement of torpedoes designed to blow up the wire. The officers were at their several stations, anxiously consulting their watches and on tension lest some unforeseen miscarriage should nullify all their plans. By ten minutes to nine the Engineers reported that the torpedoes were in position. At five minutes to nine the fuses were ignited, a train of sparks sputtered along the ground, and a series of dreadful explosions flung masses of wire into the air. The artillery opened, and the raiders, springing to their feet, dashed to their objective and disappeared from view.

But a cruel misfortune defeated the intentions of one party. The torpedoes, which had been designed to burst a pathway through the wire, were only partially successful. The outer fringes of the wire were, indeed, demolished, but a great depth still

A CITY IN CELLARS

remained uncut. To attempt to cut a way through by hand was impossible. Arrested in their course by an impenetrable barrier, the attackers could do nothing but return to their own lines.

The Black Watch, on the other hand, were more favoured. The wire, which in the case of the Gordons had resisted the explosive charge, was here gapped extensively. The raiders poured in and killed a number of Germans. They secured a few prisoners, who were unfortunately killed by hostile fire in No Man's Land. But the necessary identifications had been made, and it was now established beyond doubt that our opponents in this sector were the 1st Jagers. Le Maitre, to whose gallant example much of the success of the adventure was due, lay bleeding from deep and ghastly wounds. He was carried down tenderly to Houplines, his wounds were dressed, and he was evacuated with all possible despatch.

On the following night a dual raid, carried out by the 5th Gordons and the 6th Seaforths, achieved a larger measure of success. The Germans, in dread of a gas attack, donned

A CITY IN CELLARS

their helmets and fled in terror to their dug-outs, where they were bombed with merciless determination. A few who seemed unable to face the ferocity of our onslaught, springing over the parados, retreated with more precipitation than dignity to their support line. But they had scarcely exposed themselves so negligently in the open when they were mown down by machine guns.

Amid all these manifestations of restlessness, the division was nevertheless enjoying a repose which it was well aware would be short-lived. Already reports were in circulation that another division was on its way to our relief, that we were to proceed southwards, and that we were expected to break through on a new front or be dashed to pieces in the attempt. And when, on September 25th, we moved to Courte Croix, there was no doubt in our minds that a crisis was again near.

XI   THE GENERATION OF CAIN

ON September 27th the reports of the previous week were realised by the confirmation of the orders that we were to move southwards again. To what destination remained as yet a profound mystery. The Higher Command was uncommunicative, and one could only hazard the wildest of guesses in respect of the future. That we were likely to be more actively engaged than at Armentières, that we were not likely to be confronted with the passive belligerency of trench holding, was clearly indicated. To this end all the spare kit we possessed was flung aside and stored away, and it cut us to the heart to sacrifice so many things which by long months of usage we had come to regard as essential to our use. We carried in our valises a margin of spare blankets, and an endless supply of socks which nimble fingers had knitted at home. But the rules were inflexible, and our surplus baggage had to go. In this manner, for the second time since June, we had to jettison a large quantity of our personal belongings. But now we felt no fears of losing the discarded matter, because in the previous instance we had suffered no deprivation.

Prior to leaving for our new sphere the brigade was inspected by the Army Commander, General Plumer, a review which was interrupted by the unwelcome presence of a German aeroplane. Before it could take too close an interest in the proceedings, its curiosity was cut short by the timely arrival of a flight of our own machines, which followed hard in pursuit; but we had the mortification of seeing the intruder, after a hot chase, show a very clean pair of heels and disappear in the direction of Ypres.

A divisional billeting party had been ordered to rendezvous at Steenwerck station in anticipation of a fresh move. As the representative of the battalion, on September 27th I cycled to that place through Meteren and Bailleul, laden with four days' rations and vastly curious to learn where the Great

THE GENERATION OF CAIN

General Staff had designed to place us. The staff-captain of the 153rd Brigade accompanied us, but the other two staff-captains of the division, unwilling probably to undergo the inconvenience of travelling in horse-boxes, had decided to motor south to meet the party at Abbeville. Meanwhile our cycles were stacked in a truck and we searched for a respectable carriage, but none being forthcoming, we boarded the supply train at Calais, which was as dirty in outside appearance as the interior was greasy. I hope the supply officer will have forgiven the inspiration which seized H—— to pilfer a bale of hay and spread its precious contents on the floor of the truck and lie down thereon and be comfortable. For in very truth, accustomed as we were to filth and inured to unpleasant contact with it, yet our blunted feelings recoiled from the evil-smelling wagons into which we were crowded like so many sheep.

At 3 p.m. we lurched out of Steenwerck and crawled westwards to Calais, where we drew up near the Guines Road, and were cautioned not to move yet awhile. This halt was a military siding full of British engines, on whose tanks appeared in large white lettering the mysterious R.O.D. (Railway Operating Division). We saw so many of these locomotives distinguished in such a manner, and were so puzzled by the inability of everybody to furnish a reasonable explanation that for a very long time the glaring white letters persistently intrigued us. We did not run through Calais as we expected, but, informed that a train would be found to convey us to Abbeville the following morning, we were free to go into the town and enjoy for a few fleeting hours the pleasures of civilisation. And we were not indifferent to the primary pleasure, that of a good dinner. When we left Steenwerck, with our haversacks bulging with bully beef, we had not calculated on spending a whole night in Calais. Most of the officers disappeared into the Savage, and I did not see them again till next morning. As for myself, having dined well, and no more wisely than was desirable in the circumstances, and no less wisely than was excusable, I loitered with leisurely interest in the more social places of resort till it was time to return and secure a sleep ere the travels of the morning started in good earnest. I was perhaps the more impressed with the night scene of the Boulevard International because I had just come from scenes so different in aspect. What this patch of Calais conveyed to the every-day visitor was probably as far removed from my momentary impression of it as the one pole is from the other; and yet to me, that broad boulevard facing the docks, where the naked yards of ships loomed up in the semi-darkness, was a vivid link with the dear country across the water, and its drab colourings, faded and sad and funereal in touch with my thoughts, had a nameless charm which one cannot describe or explain away.

By great good fortune our supply train was booked no farther than Calais. More carriages, therefore, had to be attached to a military train moving south at dawn. At 6 a.m. we were given a warm cup of coffee in the Y.M.C.A. hut adjoining the siding, and exactly one hour later we rumbled slowly away, always southwards, towards the scene

THE SOMME AT ABBEVILLE

THE GENERATION OF CAIN

of active operations. We did not enter Boulogne, but skirted it without stopping, which displeased not a few of us, whose hunger had not been sufficiently appeased at Calais and now demanded satiety. A halt, however, was promised at Abbeville, and we were full of pleasant anticipations. There was a heavy mist over the Channel which prevented that eager scanning of the far horizon where the white cliffs of Folkestone sheered out of the water. At 2 p.m. we bumped into Abbeville, but, owing to a mishap to a 15-inch naval gun, we were held up for an hour just outside the station.

When at length detrainment was completed and our cycles unstacked, we dispersed for lunch to whatever restaurants suited our convenience. But refreshments had to be accelerated when instructions were issued to the officers of my brigade to rendezvous at a little place called Domqueur in two hours' time. Everybody knows the " Bull's Head " at Abbeville. I always found it packed with military men. We had an omelette or two here and coffee, and set off;

but one of the party had a puncture and was left behind.

To Domqueur, wherever that might be. The French gendarmes at the barricades had never heard of it, and shook their heads violently when we inquired for the most direct route. Some advocated one way, some insisted on another, and my map, which was a very small one, inclined me to a third; and after mature deliberation we decided to follow our own judgment in the matter. It was a long, straight, wearisome road, very hilly, for which one was not quite unprepared who possessed a hachured map of the district. It was now half-past three, and we were still about ten kilometres distant from Domqueur, with no hopes of reaching there by scheduled time if these exhausting ascents continued. To make matters worse, the weather, which had been growing increasingly sultry, now broke altogether, and there fell such a torrential downpour that we were forced to plead shelter in the nearest estaminet, which happened to be in Ailly-le-Haut-Clocher, where the outlook was philosophically discussed over a draught

THE GENERATION OF CAIN

of sour beer. The rain ceasing we climbed up to Famechon, and, still climbing, reached Ergnies.

From Ergnies we raced downhill to Gorenflos, nearly overturning a peasant woman at the mill, whose futile maledictions pursued us till we turned the corner at the church. Another slope to breast. We could see no sign of Domqueur. Some women were tending the cemetery. Where could Domqueur be, we asked. *Là-bas*, and their rough arms swept the whole horizon. A windmill was perched up on a hill before us. We toiled up towards it, and there down below in the valley lay Domqueur, enmeshed in trees, now glistening with the rains.

We arrived fully one hour late, but it mattered not, for the work of billeting was not to commence till the following morning. In the meantime the Town Major had to be interviewed in order to get house room for the night. Domqueur was already numbered, and the accommodation of each house was known. Rooms suitable for messes were recorded. I was allotted billet No. A 36 in the Chaussée Brunehaut. It was a house of very modest pretensions, but kept meticulously clean, and the good woman who lived in it, a Madame Caumartin, was kinder to me than I can express. Her husband was at the war, she having two children of her own (Eugénie being the name of one) and also caring for a third, orphaned during the course of the war.

The other officers were scattered over the village, accommodation being plentiful, as we were the only troops quartered there at the time. But we all messed together at the house of a very courtly gentleman from Amiens, whence ill health had driven him to seek a more complaisant air in the country. He reminded one very much of those pictures of the late Duke of Devonshire, with a flowing beard and features aristocratic and intellectual. His wife was a charming woman with three children, entirely lovable, Marie Louise, Madeleine, and Louis, who kissed us all good-night and good-bye, for perhaps we would never see them again, and their affectionate lispings were good to our hearts.

On the 29th the weather, which had broken down completely, surpassed all its previous efforts, and the outlook was indeed a miserable one. The prospect of impossible roads and drenching rains was none the less disturbing because we were to go into billets only three kilometres away at Franqueville, apportioned for military purposes to what was termed Area B. At 9 a.m. the staff-captain dismissed us to our various destinations.

Franqueville, which was allotted to my battalion for billets, proved to be an interminably long village, composed of wretched houses which an impartial hand seemed to have flung at random into a narrow valley, already depressed by the heavy frowns of overweening cliffs, and now much more depressed by the lowering clouds, the sheets of rain, and the muddy streams that flowed naturally into it. I flung my bicycle into the mairie, which was also the school, and asked to see the mayor, who might be able to give me some help in the task of distributing the companies. The work was finished at last and the whole battalion satisfactorily billeted—on paper.

As 2.30 I cycled back to Domqueur, for I

was both hungry and tired, and wanted to lessen the vexatiousness of the day at the fireside of the good people from Amiens with a slice of brown bread before me and a glass of wine to wash it down. Alas for such pleasant hopes! When I reached Domqueur, it was to find a motor-cyclist, covered with mud from head to foot, delivering a message to the staff-captain which made him fume outrageously. He stamped about the estaminet, frowning at the patronne till she grew frightened, and we knew by hard experience, when we were summoned to a council, that some new project was afoot of a character none too agreeable. The news was broken that the move to Area B was cancelled, and that our labour hitherto had been so much labour undertaken in vain. Had the new arrangement brooked delay, the disappointment would have been supportable. But the matter was one of extreme urgency, for the brigade was following on our heels and we had to be ready to direct them to their billets the very moment that they arrived.

After a hasty lunch we mounted our cycles

again and set off towards Domart-en-Ponthieu, following the straight Chaussée Brunehaut for the space of two kilometres, and then turning half left along a secondary road that bore us over the lip of a pronounced ridge, and finally shot us break-neck into Domart. Here we ordered tea at the Officers' Club, but before it could be served we were summoned expressly and ordered to pile our cycles and ourselves on the top of a motor-lorry for conveyance to Beauval. We left Domart by that steep road surmounting the southern bank of the valley of Gorges, within which, picturesque and peaceful, slumbered St. Hilaire. I recalled the charming days spent here in July. On through Berneuil, Fienvillers, Candas. Between Candas and Beauval, a stretch of country drearily bare of houses and trees, crowds of German prisoners were at work. It possessed a feature of great interest—one of the new narrow-gauge railways springing up between the coast and the firing line.

Considered as a billeting area Beauval was undoubtedly one of the most conveniently proportioned towns to admit within its boundaries an entire brigade. It was, besides, a town modernly equipped. It embodied a multitude of advantages hitherto unobserved. All the houses were registered, and every detail, such as barn accommodation, mess rooms, officers' quarters, transport parks, water pumps, and so forth, were noted with great precision and accuracy. It was therefore an easy task to organise the streets for the purpose of quartering the troops. It was sufficient to obtain from the Town Major a slip apportioning the streets calculated to support a battalion.

Darkness had already set in when we entered Beauval. Fortunately there was a sufficiency of time to enable us to defer our work till the succeding morning. For that night I was billeted with some others at No. 28, Rue de Haut, a house of considerable size kept by two old women, who showed us every consideration and courtesy. We had dinner at the Sable d'Or, which is near the church, an edifice of some magnificence, and the restaurant can be recommended for excellence of fare and reasonable prices. Indeed, the Sauterne turned out to be more delicious than any I had hitherto tasted. For my own personal content I selected out of a large number of good billets the house of M. Derny, the principal blacksmith. His wife was ailing and wanted quiet, and I assured the honest man that I would sleep there myself, and guaranteed that there should be no disturbance, mentally reserving to myself the right of invading some other billet if it was intended to spend the night merrily.

It was about 1 o'clock on the morning of the 30th that I was awakened from my sleep by the sound of the pipes. I started up. Surely this could not be the battalion which I was supposed to meet at Doullens station at dawn? Dressing hurriedly and stealing out of the house, I was relieved to find that they were the Black Watch, the first unit of the brigade to arrive. Had there been an alteration in train times? I asked myself this question a hundred times, and the oftener I asked it the more worried and alarmed did I become in case some untoward incident would involve me in delay and prevent me fulfilling my function as guide. But I reached Doullens long before the train wheezed into the station. When I arrived the 5th Gordons were detraining. At 5 a.m. there was a violent puffing in the semi-darkness, and a long line of wagons drew up slowly. I looked into one compartment. Ross was sleeping peacefully, and Meff was rubbing his eyes, astonished to find himself at his journey's end.

I had calculated upon a few days' rest at Beauval ere the next forward step was taken, but I had not made allowance for the wonderful organisation at work hurrying forward the preparations for the resumption of the offensive. Early in the afternoon of October 1st, while we were all chatting over coffee and making plans for spending a pleasant evening at the " Golden Sand," a preliminary order to convene billeting parties at Vauchelles foreshadowed a movement on a larger scale. Was it merely an altruistic compassion that made them turn to me with expressions of sympathy, knowing that fate had overruled my decision to sleep soundly for once at the good blacksmith's, or was it a less disinterested motive that urged them to condole with me, the luckless forerunner of their own labours? Swallowing a hasty meal I mounted my cycle, intending to abbreviate the road by crossing diagonally the rough fields adjoining the light railway, but the evil genius of the country, clogging my wheels with clay, bade fair to temporise with me. I have no doubt that this misguided attempt to save valuable time impeded, rather than accelerated, my progress.

After Beauquesnes the ground rose and fell very steeply. My comrades toiled up the incline with straining muscles, intending to rest on the top of a bare and unsightly spur, beyond which we hoped, with the assurance of visionaries, to find roads more easily negotiable. And indeed the mere beholding of Marieux, half hidden in a belt of thick woodland which flung an umbrageous *cirque* around its eastern edge, soothed in a moment the heaving of our lungs. Before Vauchelles the maidens were driving home the cattle at a lazy pace, and in the creeping darkness the sweet tinkle of innumerable bells trembled on the soft airs.

The staff-captain was impatiently awaiting

our arrival. At a hurried consultation in the gloom of a musty chamber, where the light was fed only by a guttering candle and chill draughts blew in through the chinks of the unshuttered window, the billets of the Black Watch were arranged in the neighbourhood of Vauchelles. The district was so scantily populated that quarters for the remainder of the brigade had to be requisitioned elsewhere. Darkness had by this time set in. We had no lamps, and were forced to cover those perfidious roads at haphazard, avoiding ditches by miracles and praying that our next spill would not be too uncomfortable. An hour later we descended the steep bank that overhung the southern side of the valley of the Authie, and winding among the maze of byroads came to rest at the billet of the Town Major. At Authie the necessary apportionment was decided at an estaminet which we had agreed upon as the most appropriate rendezvous for men who were weary and hungered. The patron became very obsequious when ———, the brigade interpreter, in a loud voice addressed ——— as " Mon général." Thereafter mine host continued to assure us of his most distinguished consideration. That night I slept in the " Estaminet National," in a vile bed under the tiles, which was, however, the best that the poor people could provide, being very willingly surrendered.

Meanwhile, overnight my battalion had remained in Beauval, but next day saw them again on the march. Rain commenced to fall, at first in slight showers which gave an illusory promise of dissipating, but latterly in a steady downpour. Our spirits sank to zero. We expected to meet the poor fellows drenched and ill-tempered. Drenched they certainly were, but where we looked for scowls we found smiles. By 2 p.m the battalion was making itself at home in Authie. The billets were poor but plentiful, except in the case of the officers, most of whom were cooped up in the dusty attics of the Estaminet National.

But soon there came a time when we remembered those billets, now so despised, as enchanted palaces, for we were now entering upon that stage of the offensive which entails rough bivouacs and ceaseless exposure to all the rude inclemencies of winter. During the gloomy months of October and November, when the sun did not bring a palliation of our miseries, it was only at rare intervals that a roof covered our heads. On October 4th the position of the various battalions in the brigade was altered. The 7th Gordons went into bivouac in Warnimont Wood, relieving the 8th Argyll and Sutherlands. Brigade Head-quarters remained as originally located, at Vauchelles. The 152nd Brigade, which we relieved, went into the line near Hébuterne.

Rumours of a push north of the Ancre were already being whispered. And, indeed, evidences of a coming offensive were not awanting. The artillery became more and more powerful. Guns were being massed with secrecy well maintained. Overwhelming gun power, unsuspected by the enemy, was an asset that could not be over-estimated. Tanks appeared in the vicinity, twenty-five being parked by the Louvencourt-Acheux road, the object of much curiosity. Railways sprang up with amazing speed. The proportions of the shell dumps increased visibly. The vehicular traffic was enormous, and German prisoners were being largely used to keep in repair the roads so cruelly torn by heavy motor-wagons. On all sides ceaseless preparations went on, regardless of weather, at midnight as at noon, till the safe margin of mastery was thought to be reached. It was remarkable that, although we were within measurable distance for hostile gunfire, there was no manifest activity.

One day and one night sufficed us in the execrable hutments of Warnimont Wood. We were then transferred to Louvencourt, a straggling village which had a villainous reputation for the pestilential uncleanliness of its billets and the seas of liquid mud that swamped its streets. Frightful congestion attended our efforts to secure a foothold in a village already overcrowded with troops. It was found impossible to billet the whole battalion, and the overflow was packed tightly into a temporary shelter rigged up near the horse lines. Messes were at a premium. It needed much coaxing and infinite tact to induce the patronne of the Café du Centre to let us have a room. And when she accorded us permission, it was on her own terms, by which she reserved to herself the right of introducing to the privacy of this apartment guests who were her customers. In ordinary times Louvencourt would have been assessed as a village capable of sustaining not more than two battalions. But now, when close billets were rendered imperative, accommodation had to be found for not less than the following : three battalions of infantry, signal company, machine-gun company, tank company, field ambulance, and two trains. Troops were constantly passing and repassing either to or from the line. On the 6th the 3rd Division, after detraining at Louvencourt, which shared with Acheux and Belle Eglise the honour of being a railhead to the district, moved up towards Bus.

What hitherto had been a mere rumour in the matter of an offensive now became a tolerable certainty. Who could interpret otherwise the signs of the times ? The soldiers were exercised daily in the attack, not merely on hypothetical positions, but over ground specially selected on account

HÉBUTERNE

of its physical similarity to the area that was to be the object of our future operations. Over this ground tapes were laid, skilfully representing the various German trenches as they then existed between Hébuterne and Serre. The preliminary practices were confined to the initial assault on the first four lines, the various stages of the barrage being marked by flags of different colours. When it was assumed that all objectives had been carried and the position consolidated, the imagination was called into play in supposing the transposition of the German stronghold of Puisieux-au-Mont from its actual site to that of Bus, and a sham attack was thereupon launched in order to familiarise all ranks with the besetting difficulties of the situation. In all these trials of make-believe everything that could add reality to the operation was introduced, even to the inclusion of a contact aeroplane which flew backwards and forwards reporting progress and obstacles. This systematised programme of sham fighting captured the appreciation of the keen soldier, while it quickened the intellect of the more dull. And it was clear to all concerned that no half-hearted and haphazard attack was in view, but an attack calculated to the very minutest detail.

Drafts began to swell our numbers. On October 9th our rifle strength was increased by seventy. Part of the Highland Divisional Artillery, which had been in action for a week in Aveluy Wood, was recalled. The division was girding itself rapidly for battle. How soon . . . ?

XII — AN ARMY ON LEASH

THE weather, which up to the present had been moderately good, now broke. This was an unforeseen interference. And from day to day and from week to week the projected offensive was postponed, till it was thought that it would have to be abandoned altogether. At each delay keen disappointment prevailed. The perpetual postponement of the offensive necessitated a temporary return to the original alternation of rest and duty. The trenches opposite Hébuterne were particularly vile, and suitable billets were necessary to restore our fighting efficiency when we came out to rest. But I have already shown how the few uncomfortable houses that existed were woefully overtaxed. Hereafter we were accustomed to wander about like nomads, sleeping at night in our great-coats, heavy with damp, and freezing to the clammy waterproof sheets, or clinging to each other for warmth in the huts whose porous roofs admitted the rain and earthen flooring chilled and made us miserable.

On October 8th the battalion, in consort with the other units of the brigade, shifted and took over huts in Bus Wood. Four days later, the 154th Brigade, which had been holding the line near Hébuterne, moved back on relief by the 153rd. The 152nd Brigade occupied the area thus vacated by us. We handed over the scanty equipment of the bivouac to the 5th Seaforths, our old friends of Thiepval, and moved up to relieve the 7th Argyll and Sutherlands, two companies ("A" and "C") proceeding to Courcelles, where they had an excellent choice of houses left in a good state of preservation, and the remainder bivouacking in a field near Colincamps. While the two companies billeted in the abandoned houses of Courcelles enjoyed a measure of comparative comfort, the remaining companies, as well as battalion head-quarters, were exposed to all the evil changes of weather which signalised this most execrable season. Bivouacking on the

AN ARMY ON LEASH

bare earth, under the scanty cover of tarpaulin sheets, we used to awake at dawn to find the whole countryside gripped in the rigours of hard frost. These conditions were in themselves sufficiently trying. There were more serious, if problematical, dangers overhanging. Our bivouac lay adjacent to a windmill, a solitary landmark between Courcelles and Colincamps, an ideal observation post for the artillery, as such indeed it was, and a particularly good target for enemy gunners. On every hand we were surrounded by a hornet's nest of guns, for the most part howitzers. The orchards round Colincamps were a steady blaze of fire which the Germans vainly sought to neutralise. In the low valley ground to the south of Sailly the gun emplacements were so numerous as to constitute a veritable township of life. Twelve-inch howitzers growled continually from Courcelles. A few instances occurred when the German airmen were able to evade our patrols and fly over all this ground at an altitude low enough for them to observe all that was taking place. Incidentally they could not fail to distinguish the vast array of bivouacs, however skilfully these were camouflaged. The great wonder is that, while we were there, no shell seemed to be directed at the immense reserves of men lying at the mercy of their artillery.

By both sides the greatest air activity was manifested, and a corresponding increase in artillery fighting was the result. It must be conceded that the German flying services were on this front and at this time of a very superior order. But they were bettered by our own. And no better test of air supremacy could be found than the test of comparing the numbers of the opposing observation balloons. The enemy succeeded in keeping up three before Hébuterne and Beaumont-Hamel. We had but two in immediate opposition to them; but on the far horizon the sky was scored with the trailing balloonettes of British " sausages." The number within ordinary vision was usually about sixteen—sometimes more, sometimes less. And against these, whose unwinking eyes saw everything, there was not a single foe.

I have tried to show that on this small

AN ARMY ON LEASH

front there was gradually assembling an army whose strength had not as yet been paralleled, backed by such a weight of artillery and the minor arms of Stokes guns and trench mortars, that an enemy possessed of only a very ordinary intelligence staff might well have quailed. If the Germans, looking into the future, saw the gloomiest disasters overtaking their arms, they laboured with the deadliest determination to postpone, if not to prevent, the evil. The most magnificent defences sprung up well behind their lines. And one wonders at the toil so uselessly expended upon elaborate earthworks, concreted strong points, reinforced dug-outs, and a perfect web of barbed-wire entanglements, ingeniously placed in order to impede our advance. The enemy had not only one system of defence at his disposal: he had several to fall back upon in case of necessity. He had, moreover, special assembly trenches in dead ground, where men could be massed and organised for immediate counter-attack. He was, in short, concentrating.

And we knew that he was concentrating.

AN ARMY ON LEASH

It was not unknown to us that he was hurrying up men from quieter sectors to ward off our hammer blows. The German was too methodical a fighter, too logical an opponent, to ignore all those bivouacs which his airmen daily saw increase. He could not put aside with careless indifference the fact that our 15-inch howitzers were now throwing their shattering burdens into Beaumont-Hamel, into Puisieux, into Miraumont.

Having taken over billets, or rather bivouacs, in Bus Wood as before, it was made clear to us that a new plan was in process of evolution. For we learned that the 152nd Brigade had moved south. All this gave rise to a host of rumours, some so very obviously false that they were rejected as such immediately, others so dubiously probable that we were at once plunged into controversy and argument. A statement, however, said to have been made *ex cathedra*, gained currency that the division was to take Beaumont-Hamel by storm, whose capture, as well as that of Serre, must precede any attempt at wresting Puisieux from the hands of the enemy. This view was gener-

NEAR MAILLY-MAILLET

AN ARMY ON LEASH

ally accepted as expressing the designs of the Great General Staff. A plan of such a nature was obviously *in posse*. But we might as well have tried to penetrate the mysteries of Lhasa as pry into the hidden secrets of G.H.Q. The Mystics knew their part well.

From this date onward until such time as I severed my connection with the battalion, we led a life nomadic in the extreme, never settling into an ordinary routine existence of fighting and relief, but wandering with seemingly aimless purpose from bivouac to bivouac. The life was a wretched one from the point of view of personal comfort, but we took hope from the knowledge that we were the thunderbolt in the hand of Jupiter, and Jupiter was poising himself for the throw. On October 18th we moved again, marching to Forceville, where close billets alone were available. Fairly good quarters were provided for the men. It was a much more difficult matter to find shelter for the officers. We remained, however, but one night in Forceville, and were marched forward to Mailly-Maillet Wood—into hutments falling to pieces in the last stages of decrepitude and dirt.

Mailly-Maillet Wood represented the nearest approach possible to an organised communal life. The town itself did not happen to form part of our divisional billeting area, a matter which was the cause of much regret because of the comparative immunity from damage which it enjoyed. Irreparable destruction had made itself apparent neither on the streets nor in the houses. The latter, although they bore the tell-tale marks of shrapnel, were all sufficiently intact to furnish the materials for excellent billets. Even the church, situated in the centre of the town, one might have expected to find the object of war's unsparing fury. But the church was still entire, and the façade, protected by sandbags through whose chinks the inquisitive passer-by might admire the quaint sculpture, was not disfigured by mutilation.

Two battalions were crowded into the wood fringing the southern extremity of Mailly-Maillet, viz. the 7th Gordons and the 6th Black Watch. Innumerable huts

AN ARMY ON LEASH

and tents besprinkled the sodden ground. The canvas of the tents leaked, and water oozed up from the floors and bubbled out in muddy rills. During the day rain usually fell in heavy showers, and at night, when the clouds dispersed, sharp frost set in, till we stiffened with cold as we lay trying to forget our discomforts in sleep. But he errs who thinks that the spirits of the troops suffered as the result of such trying conditions. Instead of provoking discontent, distress steeled them to endure hardships more intolerable. A strange exultant resignation set in. The misfortunes of war were accepted with stoicism. The time was coming, and it was not far off, when the thought of all these horrors would be swept away by the torrent of our impetuosity in attack.

Meanwhile what was happening to the rest of the division? The 152nd Brigade gave over its sector to the 153rd and retired for a well-earned rest to the area which we had evacuated. At this time the front line was apportioned to the storm troops in instant readiness for eventualities. Thus our brigade frontage was no more than that of a battalion, and, as later events will show, two battalions were to issue from that frontage in assault. Brigade head-quarters were at the Café Jourdain in the western part of Mailly-Maillet. The 5th Gordons, supported by " C " Company of the 7th, occupied the line facing " Y " Ravine. The 7th Black Watch were resting at Forceville, while the other two battalions remained *in situ.*

It was a matter of universal regret that the weather conditions prevailing at this time proved so unfavourable to the projected operations. For the strength of the men about to be engaged in one of the greatest and most successful combats of the war had to be wasted in the uninspiring task of repairing the trenches where the violence of the rains had washed them away and the succeeding frosts disrupted and broken down. Nearly every day gangs of about four hundred men had to be requisitioned to support this most necessary work. This fact must be taken into account when we consider the magnificent results that, in spite of physical exhaustion and the disappointment of hopes deferred, nevertheless attended the efforts of these heroes.

Mailly-Maillet Wood had a very bad reputation. It was frequently subjected to long-range shelling. There was no provision of shelters except a narrow trench that ran partially round this circumscribed area. And as the Germans usually opened upon it in the grey light of dawn, when our spirits were at their lowest ebb, these untimely outbursts were not borne without a great show of annoyance. At 5 a.m. on the 20th we were awakened from our sleep (such as it was, for the night had been intensely cold and blankets were not too plentiful) by a considerable bombardment. The shells burst in the wood with shattering noise. Splinters flew in every direction, piercing huts and tents as if they had been made of cardboard. Branches and twigs, lopped off the trees by the explosions, rained down on our heads. The Colonel's tent was twice perforated. But we had nowhere to go for security. We could only bury our heads in the blankets, ostrich-wise, and keep on hoping for the best.

AN ARMY ON LEASH

For two days the most stupendous efforts marked our attempt to neutralise the bad effects of the weather. Working parties on a huge scale were demanded and supplied. The main "up" trench, Tipperary, which began at the railway line from Auchonvillers to Mesnil, and thereafter crossed the road to Pozières (how well do I remember that blue signpost lettered "Pozières, 14 Kiloms."!) needed constant attention. The sides demanded propping. The floors required countless duckboards. Sumps were necessary everywhere to collect and drain away the water, flowing so naturally into the man-made ditches. At the same time the artillery hammered unceasingly at the German defences, giving the enemy no rest, now surprising working parties, now pounding the wire, now switching on to troops who were supposed to be resting in the rear. Particularly active was the artillery in the Ancre Valley.

On the 21st I had occasion to visit the line in order to correct existing trench maps. I mention this occasion because it opened my eyes to the tremendous preparations being

AN ARMY ON LEASH

made to ensure victory. Between Mailly-Maillet and Beaumont-Hamel scores of gun batteries, skilfully camouflaged, were ranged against the adversary. The untended fields, here undulating gently, cropped a new and dreadful harvest. On the sky-line, looking towards the east, one saw a line of solitary trees not yet ravaged. Belts of batteries blazed in the intervening space without intermission. When one gun-pit ceased to belch its flame, another took up the furious cannonade, and so all along the line the battle waged already, day after day and night after night, till the dying leaves of the woods, prematurely ageing, fluttered to earth at the quaking of the guns.

On this day was launched an attack on the slopes beyond Thiepval. From the support trench, which here overlooked the Valley of the Ancre, the eye could grasp in panoramic perspective all the frightful havoc of the Schwaben and Stuff Redoubts. White lines seamed the face of the rising ground, but the crest of it was so unutterably smashed that it was entirely white. The attack progressed. It was no indifferent barrage that swept away all opposition. In the far distance little specks of men could be seen advancing behind the protective wall as if they were on parade—regular, steady lines of them, whom no counter-shelling seemed to flurry. It was a human picture. The lilliputian dots surged forward, wave after wave, up the crest and over the top till they were lost in the clouds of dust and smoke and chalk. Prisoners soon began to be seen running out of the haze, stumbling in mad terror to escape the fury of the struggle, pitching into boggy trenches, falling into shell holes, blind to everything except the means of their own safety. A party of five was caught by a huge German shell. When the smoke had cleared away I searched long and earnestly with my glasses. No movement disclosed itself. But, what had not been there five minutes before, a rag of Bavarian kepi, flaunting its tattered red band in the poisoned air, hung on the stump of an uprooted tree.

It was impossible for the battalion to remain long where it was. As the prospect of " Z " day seemed to recede rather than

AN ARMY ON LEASH

approach, the brigade began to settle once more into the ordinary take-over routine of the trenches. The 5th Gordons, therefore, in accordance with the preconcerted programme, went into billets in Forceville, and their place in the line was taken by the 7th battalion of the same regiment. Before the operation was carried out, the men were addressed by the Right Rev. Sir G. A. Smith, Moderator of the Church of Scotland, and simultaneously a massed Presbyterian service was held in Forceville in the presence of the G.O.C. in C. Above the strains of the psalms, so grandly sung, the guns never ceased to growl. Listening to those solemn words, whose syllables were punctuated by the distant bark of the field pieces, and sometimes drowned by the earth-shaking roar of howitzers, an intense appreciation of the divine message could not fail to impress the spectator. The scene was so utterly incongruous; the persons so seemingly mistranslated: ministers from quiet Scottish pulpits to the riot of the battlefield, mud-stained fighters from the hell of the trenches to the heaven of a new congregation. Never was Assembly, even in the sanctuaries of Edinburgh, more solemn and impressive than this.

Meanwhile the bombardment of the German positions suffered no relaxation of effort to undo the effect of its destructiveness. Rather did it increase, until each morning it became customary to practise drumfire so terribly intense that one seemed to feel the earth recoiling under the mighty convulsions. The enemy's reply was invariably feeble. It manifested itself in half-hearted salvos of light shell on our supporting trenches, notably Fethard Street. He flung his weightier metal on the reserve line of St. John's Road, a trench that skirted the secondary route from Auchonvillers to Mesnil. Along this road were situated many dumps, and it is possible that these, known as they were to hostile aircraft, drew a large volume of fire. As the preparations for the attack progressed, the neighbourhood of these dumps became hourly more dangerous.

To cite an instance. There was an elaborate arrangement of supply, whereby munitions, food, and trench material in-

AN ARMY ON LEASH

tended for the use of the sector occupied by my battalion, were first unloaded at Auchonvillers, either from G.S. wagons or from special R.O.D. trains brought up at night by the newly constructed line from Acheux. They were then transported by working parties to a point selected for the purposes of distribution on account of its great convenience. This point was the junction of Tipperary Avenue with the Auchonvillers-Hamel road (which it under-tunnelled), and here battalion head-quarters were situated. The enemy learned of the importance of this position, or rather deduced its importance from various items of information brought in by reconnoitring aeroplanes and ingeniously collated by the General Staff. He began to shell it vigorously, and it acquired a notoriety which only our impulsive advance of a later date served to eradicate.

The nomenclature of these trenches differed essentially from those hitherto encountered, because they had such cosmopolitan associations. It will be recalled that not more than three miles distant a very regular system had been introduced of naming each sector after the more common topographical names consistent with the recruiting area of the brigade. Thus, *all* the trench names of "G2" sector (Thiepval), which adhered through various vicissitudes long after the fathering battalion had disappeared, belonged to Glasgow and the vicinity. Buchanan Avenue, Sauchiehall Street, Greenock Avenue, and so forth, were a lasting memorial of the 6th Argyll and Sutherlands. But here there was no similar appeal to territorial pride of appropriation. The trench names seemed to have been given at random. I cannot explain their origin. The choice in this instance does not seem to have been an arbitrary one. We found on the extreme right of the battalion that Gabion Avenue, originating somewhere near Englebelmer in the midst of countless batteries, led into Piccadilly and fed the firing line through South Alley.

Similarly, on the left, Tipperary Avenue and Broadway provided a very deep and secure footway from Auchonvillers onwards. The battalion system proper might be described as four-deep: (*a*) the firing line, (*b*) the secondary firing line, which could be regarded as a defensive line only on paper, as it was in a frightful state of disrepair and was almost completely water-logged; (*c*) the support trench, represented by Fethard Street; and lastly, (*d*) St. John's Road, whose position has already been indicated. All these trenches were so arranged that traffic was controlled with comparative ease. To this end some were designated " up " and others " down," and a third class " neutral." The arrangement was designed particularly in view of approaching battle, and certain men were detailed to ensure as thorough a control as possible when the morning of positive hostilities dawned.

We remained in the trenches but a very short time. On the evening of October 24th a change-over occurred between the 6th Black Watch and ourselves. The result was probably not to our advantage, for we exchanged dry dug-outs for the very miserable conditions of an exposed and rain-sodden bivouac. The weather was hopelessly wet. The continued depression was responsible for another postponement of our operations. But even all this precipitation could not be allowed to check the necessary preparations for the offensive. The upkeep of the trenches was still of vital importance, and heavy working parties were daily requisitioned to achieve this most essential end. At this time, however, the terrible drain on the men's energies occasioned by the need of restless supervision of all the " permanent ways " of trench warfare, and the ruthless exaction of every ounce of human labour, was not appreciated by us as it should have been. We were inclined to chafe and cavil at what we were pleased to call the crime of forcing such tasks on the shoulders of those very men who might at any moment be called upon to face the rigours and dangers of a prolonged offensive. Nevertheless, all that was demanded of us was faithfully and creditably performed. In the end we saw how necessary were all those pernicious preliminaries, and the enthusiasm which more and more was being transformed into depression by the exacting work was destined to flare up anew when the crucial moment arrived to reinvigorate and revitalise.

XIII   BEAUMONT-HAMEL

THE new bivouacs were devoid of any comfort whatsoever. Sites were laid in a clearing on the breast of a sharp incline between Mailly-Maillet and Forceville. Funkholes were dug at irregular intervals, in case the enemy opened his artillery. In the murky and rainy night, when men arrived in driblets from heavy working parties, covered with mud from head to foot, limping with fatigue, and hungry as only men are hungry when much strenuous labour is required, there were often no means of showing these wretched people the many pitfalls that lay in their path. Stumbling over the tangle of brushwood and falling into the soft oozy mud lining the bottom of the funkholes, I have heard them groping blindly for shelter, swearing roundly at everything. But I have never failed to hear them *sing* when, under equal conditions, they found a few inches of tarpaulin ready to shield them from the bitter cold or a scattering of straw to serve as their pallet. One is apt to grumble at home over little things. Let him not grumble till he has passed a night under such conditions as these.

A raid carried out with the characteristic dash of Highlanders served to break the monotony of these tiresome days. Officered by Lieutenant Lindsay, who, in appreciation of this highly successful minor engagement, was awarded the Military Cross, the raiding party left the bivouac shortly after the afternoon meal. The weather was somewhat improved, but even then not so desirable as was essential for complete success. At 5.30 the short but intense preliminary bombardment commenced. The whole operation barely lasted thirty minutes from start to finish. At 6 o'clock the signal went up, announcing the return of the raiders. During that time the salient opposite Beaumont-Hamel was penetrated, the assailants remaining unobserved till they were upon the defenders. One post of nine men was wiped out with the exception of a bespectacled

Hanoverian, called to the colours but two months before. He was very frightened and communicative. He said that his post had detected the approach of the raiders, and thought that the whole British line was advancing to the attack. Most of the Germans in the trench bolted over the parados, but were caught by our barrage and annihilated.

On November 5th the weather again assumed an aspect of the most unpromising character. "Haig's Weather" seemed to have set in: days of continuous rain, followed by treacherous intervals of sunshine, which induced the Higher Command to lay their plans provisionally. To the mortification of everybody these plans had to be abandoned time after time. When we moved into respectable billets at Raincheval, the day of the intended attack, insomuch as the barometer regulated operations, was postponed till the 10th. Little hopes were entertained, however, that the weather would hold out sufficiently long to justify the commencement of the struggle.

On the 8th it began to rain. "Z" day

BEAUMONT-HAMEL

was again postponed till November 13th. Two days later a marked improvement took place. Expectations ran high. The cannonade, which had abated slightly, was resumed with an unparalleled ferocity. The tanks were moved up from Beaussart with as little noise as possible, their approach being drowned by successive bursts of machine-gun fire. It was not considered likely that their services would be of much avail on account of the muddy soil, which tended to impede their advance. As later events proved, the tanks did not play any part in the initial attack on Beaumont-Hamel on the fateful November 13th. It is interesting to compare the fanciful and highly imaginative picture drawn in the pages of a popular and delightful illustrated weekly, showing the bloodthirsty Scots advancing on the cowering enemy under the ægis of a monster tank. Nothing was farther removed from the actual scene than this misleading representation.

It was at length decided that the weather was propitious enough for the troops to stake their fortunes on the blow projected with such consummate skill. The fervour of approaching battle thrilled everybody. Fatigues were forgotten. The complaining spirit was swept away by new and strange emotions. There is a hush in a man's soul before battle which stills the boasting utterance. It is like the frail canoe impelled by an invisible force along smooth and deep waters, with the drum of the rapids throbbing in the distance. And already the roar of the rapids grew upon the ear. On the 11th we moved into the fighting zone, bivouacking for the night near Mailly-Maillet. Now all our preparations had been completed; only the final orders remained to be issued. These were communicated to the officers about 12 o'clock noon of the 12th. It was a solemn scene. Notes of the concerted movements were taken with scrupulous care, in order that everybody, from colonel to cook, might be thoroughly acquainted with the intended plan and thus provide for a more complete victory by the assurance of individual initiative if it would be required. Suggestions were invited. The Colonel gave each suggestion its just consideration, amplifying here, rejecting there, applying that sound and sympathetic judgment of his which endeared him no less than it commanded admiration. Company commanders expressed themselves as being satisfied with the scheme of operations, and, turning to each other, interchanged wishes of good fortune for the morrow. But at least one of them was fated never to see the grand results of these painful hours of preparation.

The battalion moved off by companies at 3 o'clock on the same day, in order to take up battle position before the salient of Beaumont-Hamel. Each man wore on his left arm the distinguishing mark of his unit. Ere midnight everything had been completed for a morrow too momentous for thought. The 4th Seaforths, who had held the line while we were girding ourselves for action, filed back silently to the rear. The men to be engaged crawled up to the front, but found the jumping-off trench waterlogged. They were therefore compelled to lie behind the parados in shell-holes till dawn. Who can recall those long hours of silent vigil and freezing immobility without horror? Some warm tea and a sip of rum reached the men shivering in their greatcoats. The tea was brought up in large thermos flasks. Throughout the night an uncanny quiet settled upon the scene, and the men tried to doze, though half smothered with mud and chilled with exposure. Some to whom the blessedness of sleep, even of a broken kind, was denied, made light of their hardships. Others were moody, as if "fey." These seemed to realise that their time was at last come. The field guns uttered no warning threat yet awhile; but far away back the winking flashes in the sky and the sullen deep boom and the never-ending rustle high overhead told the tale of the heavies pouring thousands of shells into the German batteries. The hours crept on slowly, how very slowly! And as dawn imperceptibly flushed over the sky, the pulses beat quicker, awaiting the sudden deadly outburst of the field guns. At last one battery, a second too previous, barked. Then hell seemed to be let loose. Every gun spoke. An immense mine was blown on the left of our position. The earth quaked for many minutes, and an avalanche of dust and débris showered down. This was the general signal for the attack. The waves leapt forward, and in a few minutes overwhelmed the first lines.

During the night an exceedingly thick fog had banked itself over the scene of our operations, rendering useless the elaborate contact services assured by the improved methods of the Royal Flying Corps. In this blinding, enveloping veil the attacking units became inextricably involved. The single band of the 6th Black Watch showed up among the more ambitious quarterings of the 7th Gordons. These in their turn drifted unconsciously into the ranks of the Naval Division, who, stimulated by the gallantry of their leaders and straining forward to Beaucourt, bore them onwards in the impetuosity of their advance. The general trend of drift, therefore, following the local slope of the land towards the valley of the Ancre, was from north to south. The day's objective, however—portions of Munich trench—fortuitously tended to correct this natural inclination. But so densely did the mists, pooled in those miasmic depressions,

BEAUMONT-HAMEL

blot out the fiercely contested struggle from the peering vision of its immediate directors, that all the units became mere disintegrated masses, sections quitting the side of neighbouring sections, platoons splitting up into leaderless knots of wandering men, all detached and fighting with the supreme courage of isolation. The advance upon which we had staked our military reputation seemed at its very outset doomed to ignominious failure. Those fine troops who, complete in martial appointment and burning with the unselfish enthusiasm of volunteers to strike a blow for liberty, had, at the single and united instance of the subordinate commanders, calmly and without precipitate zeal disappeared into the forbidding welter-ground of desolation, were now scattered and in peril.

But the perplexities of the situation were nearly resolved at the very time when they were filling us with the greatest alarm. The fog lifted. It was now more easy to estimate how far we had penetrated, and to take instant measures to thrust home the attack. To the enemy also much of what had been obscure was now revealed. A brisk rifle fire was opened. Bombing became general. The men, possessed of the unconquerable spirit of the Highlands, were straining forward little by little towards their objectives.

Messages which had been disjointed and infrequent were now passed back in greater cohesion, and threw a much clearer light on the progress of the battle. At 8 a.m. a message from the captain commanding " A ' Company reported heavy difficulties in the way. His company indeed had been faced with the sternest task of all, the capture of the redoubtable Y Ravine, a warren of trenches under-tunnelled by a system of magnificent dug-outs. At this part hostile machine-gun fire held up the gallant advance of " A " and " B " Companies. But help was at hand. For on the right the remaining companies had pressed the enemy farther and farther, till he was finally ejected from his positions and Station Road remained in our hands. The garrison defending the ravine was now threatened from the rear, and when on the left the 152nd Brigade had carried the village of Beaumont-Hamel, its fate was decided. A company of the 4th Gordons was brought up to reinforce the waves attacking Y Ravine frontally, and by 3 o'clock the stubborn resistance of the enemy was at an end. Eight hundred prisoners fell into the hands of my battalion. The captured booty was uncountable. For many days the men lived on the immense stores of provisions taken in the German trenches. Dug-outs, deep and commodious, were found to be stocked with every kind of luxury, including wines and cigars.

All victories are won at a price. In numbers indeed our casualties were not disproportionate to the magnitude of the venture. Captain Merson fell early in the day. The two Robertsons lay dead upon the field. The murderous fighting of the day exacted a heavy toll of casualties, although the percentage of killed was low. But who shall compute the loss of even a small number of such MEN ? Their breed is invincible.